The laws of Terrorism in Northern Ireland and
pp. 103 - 115.
Britain.
esp. 109

Method of obtaining stats.

── observational   what methods of Surveys
/involvement\

Non conservative / Without Value Freedom

↓

Difficulty ~~in total~~ to remain impartial
Political involvement:

While act is produced to ~~β~~ prosecute
guilty it is more often used to
pursue the innocent ── for a no. of
reasons.

Terrorism and Criminal Justice

Terrorism and Criminal Justice

An International Perspective

Ronald D. Crelinsten
Danielle Laberge-Altmejd
Denis Szabo
University of Montreal

Lexington Books
D. C. Heath and Company
Lexington, Massachusetts
Toronto

Library of Congress Cataloging in Publication Data

Crelinsten, Ronald D.
Terrorism and criminal justice.

"This book derives from a conference entitled 'The impact of terrorism and skyjacking on the operations of the criminal justice system' held in February 1976 in Rochester, Michigan."
Includes index.
1. Terrorism—Congresses. 2. Criminal justice, Administration of—Congresses. I. Laberge-Altmejd, Danielle, joint author. II. Szabo, Denis, 1929- joint author. III. Title.
HV6431.C74   364.1   77-87185
ISBN 0-669-01983-6

International Standard Book Number: 0-669-01983-6

Library of Congress Catalog Card Number: 77-87185

Contents

List of Figure and Tables

Foreword

History bears witness to the fact that few if any nations have come into being or stayed alive without experiencing the phenomenon that is generally referred to today as terrorism. Indeed, the founders of many nations were in a state of rebellion against the then-existing order, were decried by that order as rebels, traitors, or terrorists, and were celebrated as heroes after the success of their usually patriotic missions. History also has a process of healing wounds and turning rebels into conformists and conservators of new orders. As we look at the world today, we find societies in a state of fermentation side by side with societies eager to preserve the product of their own fermentation. It is for this reason that it has become difficult to find universal agreement on how to deal with this phenomenon called "terrorism." Yet, with the ever-increasing, mass-destructive potential of weaponry at the disposition of terrorists or freedom fighters, the search for a solution has become a matter of the greatest urgency, for the threat to a tiny political entity now may threaten the peace and security of all humankind. The sympathy for the high goals and aspirations of those struggling for national independence, freedom from suppression or alien occupation, and recognition of their ethnic, racial or religious identity, cannot lead to toleration of actual or potential mass destruction on the part of those who either seek or repress these goals and aspirations. The fight for high ideals becomes heinous criminality when it wantonly destroys the values committed to the protection of all humankind in international instruments governing war and peace and securing the human rights of all human beings. The number of universally agreed upon international instruments identifying and protecting these rights is growing. Nevertheless, also growing are the attacks on these rights, and the number of tombstones marking the graves of totally uninvolved victims—men, women and children.

A few lessons seem to have been learned already. Escalation of repression leads to escalation of pressure for attainment of ideals. That escalation increases victimization of the innocent. On the other hand, removal of the underlying grievances eliminates the need to continue to fight for their removal. But the struggle of any particular group may be a long one. What can the international community do—what must it do—until that stage of bliss is reached, in order to protect the innocent and to preserve the basic human rights of the involved while the struggle lasts? Who is to decide whether any particular struggle is a legitimate striving for ideals established by the community of nations as represented by the United Nations, or whether it is a criminal enterprise in opposition to these ideals? While the phenomenon of so-called terrorism—a preferred term, at least on the international scene, might be "transnational violence"—has been with us throughout history, we have yet to learn from that history; we have yet to establish the principles by which we can deal with it.

For that reason, an effort like the present one, to study multinational experiences and to arrive at generally valid conclusions, can only be welcomed by the international community. Few would deceive themselves into believing that the problem is thereby solved. This is but a beginning, albeit an absolutely necessary first step. It does not solve the problem, but it may alert the international community to the issue and one hopes it will stimulate the scholarly community into earnest efforts appropriate to the contemporary crisis in order to preserve universally agreed upon values.

The scholars who contributed to this volume are not political protagonists. The sponsoring organization, the International Centre for Comparative Criminology, enjoys universal respect in the world by reason of the intellectual neutrality with which it has approached all issues to which it has addressed itself. This is the reason why this volume is so significant. But by sponsoring this volume, the Centre also has assumed an obligation that may take some time to complete. Through continued neutral inquiry that is detached from partisan politics, through research, inquiry, and publications, and in the atmosphere of calm that a think-tank can provide better than a political forum, the Centre must continue the search for a solution to the problem that today is derisively called "terrorism." The goal is worth pursuing: a world as free as humanly possible from terror, whether exercised under the guise of governmental authority, whether in pursuit of high ideals, or whether from base and criminal motives.

Gerhard O.W. Mueller, Chief
United Nations
Crime Prevention and
Criminal Justice Section

Note: This foreword does not purport to reflect the official views of the United Nations.

Preface

Historically, all crimes were "political," the separation of the legislative, executive, and judicial powers being a major achievement of modern statehood. One can say that nineteenth- and twentieth-century social evolution resulted in the "depoliticization" of the judicial system. This is perhaps a reflection of the growing consensus, within the liberal democratic state, concerning the essential fairness of the political machinery and the relative independence of the judicial order from it. Social democratic ideals stressing the right for a more effective equality had spread through the body politic without altering, however, the basic incentives to the exercise of individual responsibilities. The responsiveness of the holders of political power to the aspirations of the general public for material well-being and civil liberties tended to rule out violent means as a viable method for challenging the established rules of the social order.

Terrorism challenges the political system and, in so doing, represents a basic "regression" in the psychoanalytical sense. Why this regression? Why did we enter, around the mid-sixties, a period of turmoil that recalls the turbulent periods of prerevolutionary Russia, late Renaissance Italy, or the mid-nineteenth century's revolutionary years that culminated in the Paris Commune? It seems to us that we are witnessing every twenty to thirty years or so, an exacerbation of the latent opposition of world views, or *weltanschauungen.* The latest manifestations of this are the Vietnam War-induced moral crisis in the United States, the awakening of a revolutionary spirit in Paris in the spring of 1968, and the generational confrontation in Germany during the mid-sixties. All these events had in common the weakening of the value system that ultimately justifies the rule of law. The very notion of the Res Publica lost its compelling characteristics, the nature of which allowed, in the past, the smooth functioning of conflicting class, social, age, and sexual interest groups. The coherence of the system will be significantly reduced, given the growing influence of radically opposed contra-values and the militancy of those adhering to them within the same system.

We are now entering a phase of social evolution that produces a type of society in our Western democracies closely resembling the nonintegrated ideal type; opposing conducts, each having their own moral justification, are pitted against each other within the confines of a single society. Several countercultures are vying for the loyalties of the membership of a given society, and as a consequence, the sense of "civic virtues" as well as "public interest" is rapidly vanishing. And, therefore, social conflicts will exhibit tendencies to degenerate into civil wars. As Clausewitz used to say: "War is the continuation of diplomacy via other means." The same can be suggested for the use of violent means in the solving of economic and social conflicts of interest.

The contemporary criminal justice system has evolved to deal more and more with persons and less and less with acts. The problems arising from this evolution are reflected in the present crisis in "corrections": The treatment-oriented sanction related to the person does not seem to have been very effective. The terrorist as an offender looks to be the least eligible candidate for rehabilitation. This gives rise to the renaissance of the "preventive" model close to the classical school of penal law. Is this a particular development related to the "political crime" or is it a general tendency engulfing the whole criminal justice system?

Just let us recall briefly three models of crime control. The first is based on the *deterrent* effect of the sentence. The penal threat predominates, and the severity of punishment is the central piece of the strategy. The *correctional* model implies a basic trust in the ability of man to rehabilitate himself, to proceed toward a re-adaptation of his behavior to commonly accepted goals. This re-adaptation is effected by the purposeful manipulation of legal, psychological, and environmental variables. The *preventive* model stresses the consequences of an increased incapacitation of the potential offenders by reducing significantly the opportunities and capabilities to commit proscribed acts. There seems to be an increasing public resignation to the inconveniences or the price to be paid for the very expensive means required by the preventive model. The control of subways, airports, maybe even railway stations, high-rise buildings, and banks, indicates this tendency. Of course, there is, in practice, a large overlap in the effects of these three models. The deterrence model still remains rather effective for the large mass of the "silent majority"; the medical and correctional model is surely helpful with offenders demonstrating psycho- and sociopathological characteristics; the preventive model may play a significant role for the so-called "normal" or "professional" criminal.

To maintain a sense of proportion in talking about terrorism however, we should not forget the tremendous amount of violence and terror resulting from the shortcomings of the criminal justice system and its operations within our so-called "civilized" societies, not to mention wars, and so forth. Just in thinking of the twenty-five victims of the Lod airport shooting, compared to the thousands of victims of the recent Lebanese civil war, we could ask ourselves why the former made a deeper impact on world opinion than did the latter. We do not offer any ready explanation.

The frequency of terrorist acts in the recent past allows us to evaluate an increasing body of data pertaining to the effectiveness of the philosophies, strategies, and technologies used and tested by various agencies. One of the tasks of comparative criminology is to find out about particular achievements and generate a critical reflection bearing on theories and practices of crime prevention and control.

What do we want to achieve? We hope to summarize and critically evaluate the present knowledge on the subject and submit it to the international scholarly community as well as to the general public for their attention. We want to convey our concern, as criminologists or specialists in criminal policy, to have the international community look at the contemporary forms and aspects of one of the oldest of crimes: the contest for the exercise of power by violent individuals or minorities. To a large extent, this marks the end of a narrow, parochial concept of corrections and law enforcement and places them in the more appropriate and broader perspective of the political sciences.

While one sees an increasing flow of literature on terrorism as evidenced by the almost weekly arrival of new books and articles, be they technical, legal, journalistic, or fictional, the specificity of this volume lies in the perspective from which the problem is analyzed—that is, the perspective of criminal justice. By criminal justice, we mean the institutionalized form it takes in pluralistic, liberal democracies. Through their activities, the terrorists aim at demonstrating the illegitimacy, inefficacy, and inappropriateness of the present judicial and legal fabric of society. The success or failure of such an enterprise depends primarily on the responses that the criminal justice system will devise to counter these attacks. The legal framework of Western societies is characterized by complex and delicate checks and balances between the rights of individuals and the public interest, the chemistry of which can be upset both by the terrorists' actions and by the system's hasty reactions.

For the purposes of a fruitful analysis, we accept the basic premise of the criminal justice model; namely, the criminal justice system is the best available tool to guarantee equity and fairness in regulating the interaction between individual freedom and social requirements. One cannot deny that major imperfections and even inequities exist in this system and that these have to be dealt with directly. In fact, only by doing so can we gain a true understanding of the unique challenge that political terrorism poses to the democratic tradition.

The second unique characteristic of the present work lies in its comparative approach. The views and tentative conclusions of the different chapters are based on careful evaluation and confrontation of various national experiences with sometimes highly contrasting social and political histories as far as terrorism is concerned. This is especially relevant in a time when terrorism knows no boundary.

The text is organized in such a way as to bring out the unique aspects of our analysis. The first part starts from a broad perspective from which the interaction between the terrorist challenge and the criminal justice response is seen to be a reciprocal process that can be viewed as a holistic system. It then narrows the perspective and focuses sequentially on the various components of the criminal justice system and how each one is affected by the terrorist challenge. This sequential analysis culminates in a step up to the international level, which, though not in actual practice embodied in the official structure of the criminal justice system, constitutes the forefront of the struggle.

The second part deals specifically with actual national experiences in which detailed problems or cases are discussed. Thus, the overall plan of the book is to move from the broad perspective to the narrow one in order to provide the reader with several frames of reference from which to study the problem.

This book derives from a conference entitled "The Impact of Terrorism and Skyjacking on the Operations of the Criminal Justice System," held in February 1976 in Rochester, Michigan. The first three chapters in Part I, based primarily on a working paper written by R.D. Crelinsten for the conference, have been revised and updated by R.D. Crelinsten and D. Laberge-Altmejd. The remaining chapters in Part I were written by these two authors, the whole of Part I drawing on the proceedings of the conference itself. Part II, prepared by all three authors, contains edited versions of papers prepared for the conference.

R.D. Crelinsten
D. Laberge-Altmejd
D. Szabo

Acknowledgments

We would like to thank the Law Enforcement Assistance Administration of the U.S. Department of Justice and the Department of the Solicitor General of the Canadian Government whose funding made the conference, upon which this book is based, possible. Views expressed in the text do not necessarily reflect any official views of either agency or government.

We are especially indebted to all participants in the conference. Their stimulating ideas and debates were invaluable in preparing this book. We would like to extend special thanks to Bart B. de Schutter, Guiseppe di Gennaro, Edith Flynn, Tom Hadden, Louk Hulsman, Jacques Léauté, Peter Lejins, Frederick McClintock, and Jacob Sundberg, all of whom served as chairmen or rapporteurs at the conference and whose written reports were the starting point for a large portion of Part I.

While the ideas in this text owe a great deal to those expressed and discussed at the conference, the authors alone are responsible for any shortcomings of this book.

Part I:
Terrorism and the Criminal Justice System: Perspectives and Issues

Introduction to Part I

This section has a dual focus. It considers the impact of a certain criminal problem on the operations of the criminal justice system based on two sorts of questions: What effect has the problem had upon the system? What effect has the system had upon the problem? Both questions complement each other, since the answers to each one provide clues to the answers to the other. This first part is intended to provide the philosophical and methodological framework for approaching these two questions. It is not meant to be a review of current literature or a summary of current knowledge.

Chapter 1 looks at a problem that is prevalent in today's world and can be considered a criminal problem that has direct relevance to the criminal justice system. The problem is that of terrorism in all its manifest forms, including the uniquely modern one of skyjacking. Chapter 2 looks at the criminal justice system's response to the problem. The purpose of this is to determine to what extent the criminal justice system has dealt or could effectively deal with the particular criminal problem under study. Chapter 3 considers the possible side effects of the criminal justice system's response to terrorism, while the following two chapters focus more specifically on the unique problems political terrorism poses for the different components of the system. Chapter 6 examines those special difficulties stemming from the growing international character of political terrorism, and the final chapter attempts to highlight those areas of greatest heuristic value for future research.

The ultimate aim is to gain some perspective on the more general question of how appropriate and effective the criminal justice system is in dealing with *any* current criminal problem, particularly one with an international dimension such as is the case with terrorism. Thus, the specific problem of terrorism is being used as a context within which to attack the broader issues. It provides the framework upon which practical questions and realistic proposals can be based. The following chapters will delineate certain broad areas where fruitful questions may emerge and be pursued. They will also specify those areas where fruitful questions are *not* likely to emerge, either because they are sterile and unproductive areas or simply because they extend beyond the intended scope of the book.

1 Definitions and Dimensions of Terrorism

As is well known from the 1975 Vth U.N. Congress on Crime Prevention and Treatment of the Offender, which focused on, among other things, the problem of terrorism, *terrorism* is one of those terms that is easy to use but difficult to define—at least so that consensus about the definition can be reached. A brief glance at some of the appendixes in Bassiouni[1] provides a clue to the problems of definition. The first major problem area boils down to the question: Who is terrorizing whom?

The text of the U.S. Draft Convention for the Prevention and Punishment of Certain Acts of International Terrorism[2] clearly gives the impression that terrorism relates to any act, performed by an individual or group of individuals, that is designed to undermine the authority of a legitimate government or state. The Draft Proposal Submitted by the Non-Aligned Group[3] of the Ad Hoc Committee on International Terrorism concerning the definition of *international terrorism,*[4] gives the equally clear impression that terrorism is related to the suppression of personal liberties of individuals by a ruling authority or military regime.[5]

Thus, we have two opposing views of terrorism that depend on the political context of the country providing the definition. In general, well-established, developed, Western democracies are concerned with disruption of societal functioning by persons engaged in terrorist activity against the state, while relatively new, "underdeveloped" countries, often founded on the basis of revolution or protracted guerrilla activity, are concerned with oppression of indigenous populations and suppression or restriction of the freedom of dissent by repressive governments.[6]

How can these two views be reconciled? An attempt to do so is certainly an important issue. Are, for example, these opposing views of terrorism a reflection of a "generation gap" between nations? A research project on the parallels between the development of people from innovative, exploratory, radical adolescents into traditional, habitual, conservative adults and the evolution of new, revolutionary, developing nations into old, history-bound, bureaucratic nations might be of immense value in this regard, but the methodological problems would be considerable.

Even though we will not attempt to resolve the conflict between the two opposing views of terrorism in this discussion, both perspectives must be kept in mind. To avoid confusion, we will view terrorism mainly from the first perspective—that is, individuals or groups of individuals acting against the interests of the state or the status quo of modern society. The latter perspective involving suppression of individual liberties by governments will be viewed as one of the dangers or "social costs," to use Minor's term,[7] that must be seriously considered as an integral part of the problem of combatting terrorism. This issue will be considered in more detail in Chapter 3.

The second major problem area involved in the definition of terrorism centers on the question: What is the relationship between terrorism and warfare? Jenkins[8] makes the intriguing point that terrorism may be evolving into a type of surrogate warfare. New disclosures since the 1975 OPEC kidnapping in Vienna suggest that this evolution has in fact begun to occur. The OPEC incident is now believed to have been planned by the governments of three nations (Algeria, Iraq, and Libya) and the action to have been directed against the government of Saudi Arabia. Thus, governments are now using actions often considered as terrorist actions to influence other governments. Whether the actual kidnapping should be considered an act of terrorism or simply a type of international extortion is an interesting question.

This problem area includes a concern that has direct implications for the second focus of this volume, the criminal justice system itself. If terrorism is viewed as a type of surrogate warfare as Jenkins suggests, then there may be profound implications for the role of the criminal justice system in dealing with it. There is a whole body of international law related to warfare; certain criminal acts are no longer treated as such during warfare (at least, until recently, by the side to which the perpetrator of the act belongs); acts of war are dealt with by defense departments and armed forces, not criminal justice systems and police forces. While a detailed examination of these implications will not be made here, the issue should linger in the back of one's mind, especially when considering the social cost of combatting terrorism via the criminal justice system. If police departments become armies, who will carry on traditional police functions? Pointing out the fact that the current trend in law enforcement is toward "special units" for special criminal problems emphasizes the increasingly numerous tangents along which a discussion of the implications of terrorism for the criminal justice system might be drawn.

The third problem area, which is related to the definition of terrorism as warfare, involves the question: What are the international aspects of terrorism? As mentioned at the outset, terrorism can be viewed as a criminal activity. As such, it can be carried on within a nation or between nations. We get into the problem area in deciding when to define a terrorist act as an internal (intranational) problem and when to define it as an international problem. Interestingly, Green[9] *excludes* the following types of incidents from the scope of *international* legal control of (international) terrorism:

1. The terrorism of the IRA in Northern Ireland, which he considers to remain within the domestic jurisdiction of the affected state;

2. Terroristic acts directed by governments against their own citizenry;
3. Ordinary activities of the active revolutionary or political dissident;
4. Acts of violence serving purely private ends, for example, kidnapping.

Depending on how international terrorism is defined, different laws can be applied and a given terrorist act can fall within the jurisdiction of different legal institutions. Clearly, the political considerations of the country providing the definition are involved here, as was the case in the earlier discussion on who is terrorizing whom.[10] The "internationalization" aspect is also relevant to the dual focus of this discussion to the degree that it has an effect on the criminal justice system's attempts to deal with the terrorist problem. Given the difficulties of international cooperation, we can perhaps argue that to consider solutions—such as the establishment of an International World Court[11]—that depend on cooperation would be an exercise in futility or naivety. On the other hand, such an issue as the effect of the international aspect of terrorism on criminal justice operations with an international focus, such as extradition, might be a more fruitful area for consideration. Both topics will, however, be discussed in Chapter 6.

The final major problem area in the definition of terrorism concerns its historical context and entails the question: What makes terrorism so special today? We can find the answer by looking at what unique elements characterize our modern society, for even though terrorism has existed as a form of criminality for centuries, it has undergone as radical an evolution as the context in which it now occurs. In terms of our dual approach, the most obvious of the elements in modern society that have an impact on terrorism itself and on the criminal justice system's response to it are the great technological advances that have given man undreamed of control over his environment. At the same time that we have gained this extraordinary power, we have created, and continue to create, those very tools which can be used against us. Sophistication breeds vulnerability.

The effects of this technological sophistication can be seen in the nature of the targets chosen by terrorists, by the weapons they use, and by the methods employed to counter their acts. Perhaps the most obvious example of a technologically sophisticated target is the modern airliner or the jumbo jet. Other potential targets include communications systems and nuclear power plants, both of which represent two of the most characteristic technological advances of our modern age. Moreover, we can consider urban water reservoirs and sewage systems, hydroelectric plants, offshore oil wells, gas and oil pipelines, and submarine cables as other attractive targets for terrorists who want to avail themselves of the latest developments in technological vulnerability. Although the weapons used by terrorists usually include handguns, grenades, and home-made bomb devices, plastic explosives and portable rockets are examples of the technologically changing character of the terrorist's arsenal. Finally, the use of electronic screening devices at airports is the best example of technological advance in counterterrorist measures. The use of closed-circuit television is another example.

The increasing utilization of new and more sophisticated technologies has contributed to the spreading involvement of more and more countries in single terrorist incidents. This international trend of modern terrorism is partly a function of the increasing interdependence of the world community that has been brought about by the very same technologies that increase vulnerability to terrorist attack, namely, travel and communications. Modern media technology, most notably television and radio, has increased the potential for gaining the necessary public attention and creating the atmosphere of fear and uncertainty that are key objectives of the terrorist strategy. We only have to look at some of the more sensational skyjacking or international hostage incidents to see that more and more countries are involved in individual incidents and that the impact of each incident reaches across national boundaries and geographic barriers instantaneously to gain a wider and wider audience. Such publicity would have been impossible in earlier eras.

Modern technology becomes a problem area insofar as the exponential growth of travel and communications has forced us to continually re-adapt our perception of the world, our *weltanschauung*. Despite a persistent parochialism in our identification of communities, as evidenced by the current wave of nationalism, we cannot stop our world from shrinking. The global village is a *fait accompli*. The aims of terrorism and the response to it are inextricably bound to this phenomenon in two particular ways. First, we can no longer ignore the economic, social, and political differences and inequities that exist throughout the world—that is, the differences between the "haves" and "have nots," the need for universal justice, and a world social order that prompt much of the terrorist action. We cannot push these problems away and isolate them in distant corners of the globe since the boundaries of our society now embrace the entire planet. Second, we can no longer afford the luxury of thinking of terrorists as Martians or as some alien problem "out there." "Elsewhere" does not exist anymore: In the global village, terrorists are our neighbors.

Unfortunately, the advances in technology that have led to this situation have not been paralleled by comparable advances in political, social, and moral awareness. This disparity has generated new problems such as the technology gap that has resulted in a hierarchy of nations that has evolved to such a point that we are now beginning to talk about a "Fourth World." This same disparity also exacerbates the existing problem of terrorism itself. The social, political, and moral immaturity that is so evident in contrast to modern technological sophistication is characteristic of both those in power and those seeking power through terrorism. Whether the focus is on the maintenance or the overturning of the established social order, the focus is often exclusively on the use of more and more sophisticated technology.

Thus, the tendency to speak of a "new wave" of terrorism or the "modernization" of terrorism is in fact quite apt. However, to talk about terrorism as if it were some homogeneous phenomenon is merely to recognize a problem area and nothing more. For one thing, as we have seen, terrorism means different things to different people, and these variations themselves reflect the many areas in which terrorism is a problem that affects the operations of the criminal justice system. There is a need to be precise about the different kinds of terrorism that occur if any progress is to be made in criminological theory and preventive practices that focus on the root causes of the problem rather than the use of technological counter strategies. While we cannot promise quick and easy solutions, we can at least try to better understand the complexities involved. One way of doing so is to identify the various possible dimensions of terrorism that might facilitate a meaningful classification on which to base future research. In this regard, we can point to the following four perspectives: the motive dimension, the spatial or geographical dimension, the temporal dimension, and the sociopolitical dimension.

The first of these needs very little explanation as it is one with which everyone is very familiar. The *motive dimension* ranges from the politically motivated person all the way to the one whose exclusive objective is financial gain such as the professional criminal. The nonpolitical end of the spectrum includes those persons who are motivated by personal revenge, a craving for publicity, a desperate attempt at egoboosting, or whatever other reason internal logic might provide. Apart from the clear-cut poles of politically or nonpolitically motivated terrorists, there lies a vast array of hybrids whose exact parentage is difficult to pin down. This group would include terrorists whose precise political stance is never made explicit or whose choice of criminal activities does not seem very relevant to the political purposes they otherwise put forward. Interestingly, such groups as the Ku Klux Klan in the United States or the Mafia in Sardinia and Sicily tend to be regarded by the existing authorities as criminal elements rather than political terrorists, even though many of these groups pursue goals having definite political connotations. Another variation would be those criminals who, for one reason or another, utilize political terrorist groups or hide behind a façade of political rhetoric, either to further their own personal aims or to get out of a sticky situation. Bank robbers who turn into revolutionaries when caught in the act are an increasingly common example of this last type.

The expression "international terrorism" points to the essence of our next dimension. To define an act of terrorism properly on our *geographical or spatial dimension,* we must take two parameters into account: site and target. If we assume that the terrorist is working for his own cause, site and target can each be viewed in only two ways: The terrorist's *own* domain or a domain *other* than his own. Table 1-1 depicts the kinds of terrorism that result.

Examples of purely internal terrorism would include most activities of the

Table 1-1
Terrorism Classified by Geographical Location of Act

		Target	
		Own	Other
Site	Own	internal (domestic)	international
	Other	external	international

IRA, the Laporte kidnapping of 1970 in Quebec, activities of the Tupamaros in Uruguay or the ERP in Argentina, when directed at their own officials. The distinguishing characteristic of external terrorism lies in choice of site. The most typical cases of external terrorism involve attacks on officials of a terrorist's own country, most notably diplomats, who are residing abroad. An example would be the Baader-Meinhof attack on the West German embassy in Stockholm in 1975. To be labeled "international," a terrorist act must involve a country or jurisdiction other than that of the terrorist. There are many examples of this type of terrorist activity, including most of the recent spectacular skyjackings and kidnappings of foreign diplomats.

The international aspect of the geographical dimension is further reflected in the increasing degree of cooperation among separate terrorist groups so that, more and more, individual incidents are jointly planned and implemented by persons of diverse national backgrounds. While we have assumed up to this point that terrorists are acting in their own interests for the causes embraced by their own particular organizations, more and more groups are not limiting themselves to such personal aims, as evidenced by the increasing amount of cooperation among established terrorist groups. Thus, a new type of terrorism is emerging: A terrorist group originally identified with a specific purpose will assume, at least temporarily, the goals of another such group. *Transnational terrorism* is becoming the generally accepted term for this phenomenon. Two of the best known groups engaging in such activities are the Japanese Red Army (e.g., the Lod airport massacre of 1972) and the Baader-Meinhof group.

By the *temporal dimension*, we simply refer to whether a particular action is planned in advance or not. At one end of the spectrum, we have well-organized, well-executed operations, such as many kidnappings or the March 1977 multiple hostage situation in Washington. On the other end, we have spontaneous actions, enacted on the spur of the moment in reaction to unexpected threats or opportunities. In view of the motive dimension previously mentioned, the spontaneous kind of action can usually be expected to occur in nonpolitical situations. This is not to say, however, that a political terrorist will not resort to spontaneous action, particularly if a previously planned action goes awry or if an unexpected opportunity presents itself.

The final perspective we wish to examine actually includes two dimensions, the interaction of which can be embodied in a concept of *sociopolitical equilibrium*. First, we shall consider the social organization that characterizes a given society, which we shall refer to as "order." The second dimension, termed "power," looks at who holds the "reins of command" of a given society—that is, who is in charge. Our purpose is not to analyze in detail the workings of these phenomena per se, but to look at them exclusively in terms of what the terrorist hopes to accomplish: change or maintenance? More explicitly, in terms of "order," the terrorist can aim to change or to maintain the existing sociopolitical organization. As for "power," the aim of a terrorist group could be to take over the reins of power or to help those already in power (to which they usually belong themselves) to keep hold of their position.

Table 1-2 illustrates the different types of situations which can arise out of the interaction of these two variables. We should note that this system applies best to large social organizations, such as countries, and as the table clearly shows, terrorism can embrace the more covert activities of established governments as well as the more obvious activities of traditionally defined subversive groups. When viewed in this way, these sociopolitical dimensions can be applied to our earlier concern, in defining terrorism, with the questions of who is terrorizing whom and when to consider terrorist activity an intra- versus international problem.

The components in Table 1-2 also make clear how these dimensions can be related to the warfare definition of terrorism. We can therefore understand why the war analogy is so popular, both in law enforcement circles and among the terrorists themselves. This analogy is clearly reflected in some of the names by which terrorist groups choose to identify themselves, for example, the Japanese Red *Army* or the Irish Republican *Army*. Also, the title of specialized law enforcement groups trained to deal with terrorism—for example, Special Weapons and Tactics (SWAT)—tend to convey this military flavor. The invocation of the War Measures Act in Canada during the FLQ crisis of 1970 is an example that clearly demonstrates how the war analogy can be applied to the control of

Table 1-2
Possible Outcomes of Sociopolitical Equilibrium

		Power	
		Change	Maintenance
Order	Change	revolution	cultural revolution
	Maintenance	separatist movements coup d'état	totalitarianism

terrorism by established authorities. Finally, the discovery of SA-7 rockets in the possession of Arab terrorists at Rome airport in 1973 and the use of sophisticated bazookas at Orly airport in 1975 are examples that attest to not only the military character but also technological advances in terrorist weaponry.

The preceding discussion makes quite clear that the greatest challenge that terrorism poses for the criminal justice system stems from its sociopolitical dimension. For this reason, the following chapters, which focus on the criminal justice system, will deal primarily with modern political terrorism. Skyjacking is the clearest example of the definitional issues and dimensions of modern terrorism presented in this chapter. The nature of the target, the weaponry used, the multiple jurisdictions involved in international flights, the transnational character and motivations of the groups attempting skyjacking, and the sociopolitical equilibrium surrounding various attempts all reflect the elements of modern terrorism and the issues involved in combatting it via the criminal justice system.

The word *skyjacking* is itself new, but it derives from an older, well-known word: *hijacking*. Thus, the nature of the crime is old but the specific context is new. Because of its unique role as a "new form of criminality," skyjacking has lent itself quite nicely to paradigmatic treatment, where it has been used as a case study for criminal justice attempts to control a particular problem. Attempts to control skyjacking have forced the criminal justice system to shift its traditional crime control model from one of deterrence and/or rehabilitation to one of prevention. How, when, and where the phenomenon of skyjacking affected the criminal justice system in this way and how, in turn, the criminal justice system affected skyjacking will be discussed in the next two chapters. In terms of our dual focus, we could not ask for a better case study.

2 The Issue of Prevention

If we wanted to state the goals of the criminal justice system in the widest possible terms, the result would likely be in terms reminiscent of the title of the Vth U.N. Congress: Prevention of Crime and Treatment of the Offender. We all would probably agree that crime should be prevented—although as we have seen in Chapter 1, in the case of terrorism we could argue about what constitutes the crime—and that offenders (the modern word for criminals) should be treated—although we might argue about what constitutes treatment, let alone offenders. The question is *how*? In the world of theory (ideas) anything is possible, but in the world of practice (actions), this is not necessarily so. For this reason, academics and practitioners seldom communicate in a productive manner with each other; researchers and policymakers frequently come into conflict with each other.

In a forum where academics, practitioners, and policymakers meet under the same roof to discuss common problems, one can very quickly come face-to-face with this polarization of perspectives. However, the dual focus inherent in the topic under consideration should obviate the necessity for a sterile confrontation since the nature of the topic is such that both perspectives should complement each other. Theoretical issues usually derive from practical experiences, while practical strategies usually derive from theoretical notions.

Academics, practitioners, and policymakers can all gain something from considering one specific problem from different perspectives, and they can all clearly benefit one another in doing so. In fact, this book is designed to facilitate this process, and because of its unique role as a recent, discrete, and well-studied phenomenon, skyjacking has been singled out as being highly relevant to this issue. The response to skyjacking was not necessarily the direct application of a conscious change in a working model or theory; it evolved that way simply because earlier efforts failed and the problem continued to get worse. Terrorism in the form of skyjacking clearly had an impact on criminal justice strategies of crime control, and the resulting shift in strategy has direct implications for both theory and practice. Consider the following scenario.

A new criminal problem appears on the scene. For political reasons, it is not viewed as criminal. Green[1] discusses how the criminal element of early skyjackings in Eastern Europe was ignored in the light of the political context, as was clear in judicial rulings on extradition. The phenomenon spreads and mushrooms. The criminal justice system responds in various ways. There is public outcry; international conventions are held (Tokyo, 1963; The Hague,

1970; Montreal, 1971). Psychological profiles are developed for screening procedures. Sky marshalls are used in the United States. Finally, after a sensational media event (Munich, 1972), mandatory luggage inspection with technologically sophisticated equipment is instituted in the United States. The incidence of skyjacking falls dramatically to zero.

The story is a remarkable one and reflects an evolution in the criminal justice system response to skyjacking that moved through several distinct phases. Herein lies the marriage between theory and practice. The skyjacking case shows how the prevalent offender-oriented crime control models of deterrence and rehabilitation were found to be ineffective and inapplicable, respectively. The criminal justice system was forced to adopt a new model—a model that focused on the environment in which the criminal act occurred rather than on the perpetrator of the act or even on the act itself. Minor deals with skyjacking as a case study for criminal justice attempts to control terrorism and describes this "prevention model"[2] that focuses on diminishing opportunities to commit acts in the first place. Designing an environment in which the specific criminal act cannot occur in the first place has literally "prevented crime." Furthermore, there have been no offenders to be treated!

Robert Hamblin and Jerry Miller have also used skyjacking as a case study that lends itself well to theoretical treatment concerning fluctuations in social phenomena.[3] They show that, during the past decades, skyjacking has occurred in discrete "epidemics" and that social reaction, represented by deterrence and policy attempts, has exhibited a similar pattern with a degree of lag. Hamblin and Miller define *deterrence attempts* as "any publicized actions by passengers, airline personnel, or authorities which, if successful, might increase potential hijackers' expectations of failure and punishment."[4] They cite as examples the publication of incidents in which skyjackers are subdued and arrested, talked into surrendering, shot, detected before boarding the airplane, or tried and sentenced. They also cite extradition agreements concerning skyjacking and the implementation of search and detection procedures as other examples. *Policy attempts* are defined by Hamblin and Miller as publicized actions by those who attempt to influence policy related to the response to skyjacking or the treatment of skyjackers. They point out that such publicized actions are usually directed toward the airlines or the national and international agencies that have the official responsibility for controlling skyjacking. They cite the following as examples: letters to the editor, newspaper editorials, legislation, threatened or actual boycotts by pilots' associations, public announcements of the implementation or curtailment of specific control efforts, and reports on the negotiation of international agreements.

Hamblin and Miller also suggest that a vicarious learning process occurred on both sides whereby skyjackers on the one hand and those who combat them on the other each learned to be more effective from the pattern of success and failure exhibited by their predecessors. Accordingly, two parallel learning processes were going on in concert that led to the evolution of more sophisticated and dramatic forms of skyjacking and the evolution of more effective ways of combatting skyjacking. The implications of this double learning process for the practitioner seem to be that attempts to control certain criminal phenomena should take into account the temporal aspect of these phenomena. They are not static and neither can the process of control remain static—at least until effective control has been achieved—which means that practitioners should be aware that skyjackers are learning from their own mistakes just as the practitioners are learning from theirs. Ultimately, effective control is achieved when skyjackers do not even get the chance to make mistakes, let alone succeed.

While Hamblin and Miller do not consider the possibility of skyjackers and their opponents learning from each other's successes and failures rather than their predecessors', the possibility of such a learning mechanism is intriguing. In fact, the successes on one side should tend to coincide with the failures on the other, although this is not necessarily so. Both sides can fail, or a strategy that succeeds at one time can fail the next time because the other side learned something and changed its strategy accordingly.

If, however, such a feedback mechanism exists between those who act and those who combat the action, it has direct implications for the control strategy. For example, the theoretician can ask what factors facilitate or retard this feedback mechanism (e.g., press reports may facilitate the process, as may "do-it-yourself" books on bombs, and so forth). Practitioners, once aware that such a process exists or may exist, can take into account the "information effect" of their practical applications. Interestingly, the deterrence strategy is suddenly cast in a new light by the possibility of this two-way learning process. While, for example, a Sky Marshall Plan may be publicized primarily for a deterrent effect, the message may not be taken that way by the "other side." In fact, terrorist strategies may be modified to accommodate the contingency of armed personnel on airplanes even if, in actuality, such personnel do not exist or exist in very small numbers. Thus, the knowledge that a two-way learning process may exist allows strategies and policies to be evaluated from the double perspective of intended goal (by the criminal justice system) and perceived goal (by the terrorist).

The implications of this double process are relevant to both theoreticians and practitioners for they provide insights into the nature of crime control and the role of the criminal justice system in this process. For the theoretician, the case of skyjacking shows how the criminal justice system's response to a burgeoning problem could be systematized into different control models. In terms of the impact of skyjacking on the operations of the criminal justice system, we could argue that the "epidemics" of skyjacking forced the criminal justice system to find a method of crime control that was different from the prevailing ones. For the practitioner, the skyjacking case provides a successful strategy of crime control that can now be tried out on other problems.

As outlined above, the case of skyjacking provides an example where the prevention of a particular criminal activity was achieved by what is often called "target-hardening."[5] This idea is predicated on the notion that certain criminal acts are more easily prevented by acting on the targets of such acts than on the potential actors. A parallel in the realm of auto accidents and resulting deaths and injuries is the case where, instead of deterrents aimed at speeding and drunken driving, the focus is on collapsible lampposts and elimination of concrete median strips. Oscar Newman's book[6] on "defensible space" applies the concept to city design and crime prevention whereby communities are designed to eliminate those environmental factors that are known to be conducive to criminal activity, for example, secluded streets, shaded areas, and so forth.[7]

One of the most obvious results of a model of crime control that focuses on the environment and attempts to prevent crime from happening in the first place is that, theoretically at least, the number of offenders would decrease drastically. If the concept of target-hardening and environmental design are coupled with the current emphasis on community involvement in preventing crime at its source and with the legal concept of decriminalization, then we get a picture of a crime prevention program that is concentrated on the extreme left of the classic criminal justice system organigram.

Figure 2-1 depicts this trend at various stages in the criminal justice process. The focus shifts from "after-the-fact" models, such as rehabilitation or treatment, to "before-the-fact" models, such as prevention or deterrence. While prevention is an act-oriented model, deterrence is an offender-oriented model. The inefficacy of the deterrence model for certain types of offenses, including most acts of violence, as opposed to its efficacy for offenses such as traffic violations or shoplifting, suggests that the impact of terrorism would be consistent with a shift from offender-oriented models to act-oriented models. Furthermore, the rehabilitation model—an "after-the-fact," offender-oriented model—would likely be inapplicable to a convicted terrorist, whose offense is often motivated by a desire to overthrow the public authority of which the criminal justice system is a part—that is, unless brainwashing is to be included in a rehabilitation model, which is a moot point.

Thus, in terms of our dual focus, we see that terrorism would force the criminal justice system to shift its crime control models to one that focuses on the act rather than the offender and, consistent with this, to direct its efforts on conditions *before* the act rather than after an act is committed. In turn, the proven effectiveness of such a prevention model in the case of skyjacking has broad implications for crime control in general and terrorism in particular.

The first of these implications is related to the current debate within the criminal justice system over the future of the rehabilitation and treatment models. If more effective crime control can be achieved by preventive strategies, pouring financial and personnel resources into new correctional institutions or

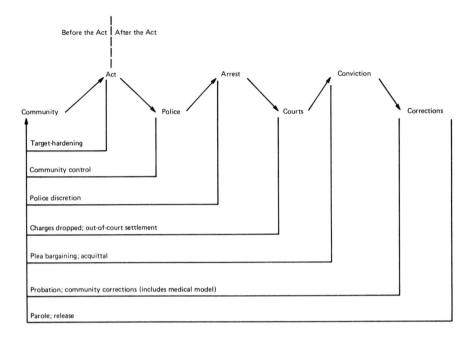

Figure 2-1. Examples of the "Leftward Trend" from Various Components of the Criminal Justice System to the Community. Control models focused *before* the act are consistent with this leftward shift.

programs may be unnecessary. Such a shift in policy would also be consistent with the current "diversion" trend from the criminal justice system toward the community. However, as pointed out at a Toronto Crime Prevention Workshop, "in many cases the community appears to be more retributive (punitive) than the criminal justice system,"[8] and accordingly, the criminal justice system, with its concepts of "due process" and "equality before the law," is better equipped than any community system to deal with crime control. The opposing view was also made at the workshop:

... [the more punitive attitude of many communities] is perhaps because the community generally has so little experience in dealing directly with the problems of crime under our current system.... [but] with practice and experience in taking responsibility for dealing directly with many of their own crime problems, communities would adopt less punitive, more humane, and more functional solutions to crime problems.[9]

Within the realm of terrorism, Clutterbuck[10] makes the point that much of the responsibility for controlling terrorism can be assumed by the public-at-large, or at least more than is generally imagined. He suggests various things the average citizen could look out for, for example, suspicious packages or strangers loitering in residential areas. By being aware of the problems terrorists face, the average citizen can maintain some degree of vigilance for certain telltale signs that could imply preparations are being made for a terrorist action. Clutterbuck also suggests that persons who are likely targets for kidnapping attempts can make things more difficult for the potential terrorist simply by changing their routines constantly. Thus, community involvement in crime prevention and control is clearly relevant to the specific problem of combatting terrorism.

The second implication of the prevention model's successful shift of focus from the offender to the offense is related to legal sanctions for acts of violence. Green[11] points out that a double standard often exists concerning the way violent acts of individuals are viewed: If the perpetrator's political motivations are looked upon favorably, the person is considered a patriot, a freedom fighter, or, if apprehended and/or executed, a martyr; if, on the other hand, the perpetrator's political motivations are not looked upon favorably, the person is considered a traitor, a bandit, or a terrorist.

This double standard appears throughout history and is reflected in many of the popular legends that derive from historical fact. Robin Hood is one example of a folk-hero-to-some-but-a-bandit-to-others. Many sea pirates were admired by some people and were romanticized in popular ballads, but, they were feared and hated by others. Napoleon is depicted as a tyrant and dictator in English history books, but appears as a hero and emperor in French history books. Even Astérix, the French comic book character, is an example of this double standard. To the French readers (the historic descendants of Gaul), he is a hero, while to the Romans, at least in the comic books, he is a renegade and "terrorist." Che Guevara is probably the best modern prototype.

Green feels that by focusing on the act and not the offender, the double standard can be avoided:

Any attempt to cope with terrorism must be directed to the act rather than the actor, so that sympathy for those who commit the alleged terrorist act must not be allowed to invalidate condemnation of the act.[12]

The prevention model is clearly effective in defusing the "martyrability" of the convicted terrorist. By focusing on the act and not the motive, the tendency to lionize the offender is minimized. In conjunction with the emphasis on target-hardening, anyone who breaks the preventive screen, so to speak, will be treated in a similar fashion—that is, as a "common criminal." From this perspective, the best course of action for the criminal justice system would be to minimize legal sanctions for terrorism per se and simply to use the more traditional offenses such as murder, manslaughter, extortion, or kidnapping as the basis for disposition.

Green makes a distinction between preserving the rule of law (action should be taken regardless of motives) and mitigating circumstances in the matter of punishment. This attitude is consistent both with the prevention model's shift of focus from the actor to the act itself and the environment in which it can or cannot occur and with the perspective that all violent acts be dealt with on equal terms. Motives and circumstances can be taken into account and discretion can then be applied in the ultimate disposition of the offender. Harsh sentences can be applied to repeat offenders or those who inject their criminal acts with morally reprehensible or emotionally repugnant zeal. The increasing victimization of "noncombattants" in the terrorist context can also be a factor here. Lighter sentences or even probation can be applied in cases such as the naive youth seduced into a terrorist movement by sophisticated ideologues or the person who committed acts out of fear of reprisal or as a result of intimidation by other members of a group. Other types of discretionary action that can be applied are directed less at the attendant circumstances of the particular case, but are more in the nature of acts of expediency. Thus, probation or some token sentence with early parole would be applied in recognition of the fact that the convicted terrorist, once institutionalized, could become the object of further terrorist activity designed to obtain his release. Further pragmatic reasons for lighter sentencing could be that the convicted terrorist would be a disruptive element in a prison community, that the terrorist's integration, particularly in the case of a foreigner, into the prison community would be impossible, that strong antiestablishmentarian views on the part of the terrorist make the possibility of rehabilitation minimal. (Some of these issues will be explored in greater detail in Chapters 5 and 6.)

The third implication of the proven effectiveness of the prevention model relates to the potential applicability of target-hardening to other pressing criminal problems. At least in the United States, there is still a sterile controversy raging over a similar and long-recognized preventive strategy for armed assault and armed robbery—the registering (at least) or restriction of availability of all handguns. Perhaps in the light of the success of the skyjacking case, more attention will be paid by policymakers to the implementation of strategies that focus on the act and the environment in which it occurs. A similar approach in dealing with modern terrorism, would be to reduce the availability of certain weapons. In light of this comparison and in view of the "technological advances" of modern terrorism discussed in Chapter 1, Jenkins' comment about terrorists' "Saturday Night Specials" being hand-held, laser-guided missiles, rather than the traditional revolver,[13] is clearly neither flippant nor irrelevant. Within the realm of terrorist acts other than skyjacking, whether similar successes can be achieved in controlling, for example, letter bombs and other types of bombing or kidnapping, is an open question.

Thus, one effect of the success of the prevention model in the case of skyjacking may be to stimulate research into the specific problem situations where it may be successfully applied. In a broader sense, one of the potentially most fruitful areas of research, especially on an international level, would be to compare different experiences with the prevention model to see whether its applicability is indeed general. At the same time, however, research is needed into issues and problems raised by overenthusiastic application of the target-hardening approach.

One such problem, which was raised by Minor[14] and also mentioned in the Toronto workshop proceedings in the section on law reform, is the problem of crime displacement. When control efforts reduce the incidence of a particular criminal activity to zero, has the crime really been "prevented" or has it merely been displaced into a new dimension? In the case of skyjacking, Minor points out that the incidence of helicopter and private plane hijackings has increased since full airport screening went into effect. Also, we can point to the 1975 hijacking of a train in Holland as a new form of the same game. This issue of crime prevention or crime displacement is intimately related to policy planning in terms of commitment of resources—financial and personnel. If crime is merely being displaced, is investing money and personnel in a specific area of crime prevention worthwhile? This question will be integrated into a more global perspective in the next chapter, which examines the impact of terrorism on various components of the criminal justice system and the social costs of combatting it via the system.

3 The Impact of the Response to Terrorism

As we have seen in Chapter 2, the criminal justice system response to skyjacking is a good example of the relatively new concept of "target-hardening" or, as Minor[1] calls it, the crime prevention model (as opposed to the deterrence or rehabilitation models). From the perspective of preventing the specific criminal activity, the plan is very effective: The incidence of skyjacking incidents in the United States fell to zero upon implementation. While we have already mentioned the problem of crime displacement—terrorists shift their attention to softer targets—we must also consider the effects of this new strategy on other aspects of the criminal justice system. For example, there is the legal issue of the right to screen passengers. Although new laws can be written or old ones modified to accommodate this new and effective procedure, there are problems such as the setting of legal precedents or the application of a new law to situations for which it was not originally intended. If drugs are found during a search for weapons, can charges for drug traffic be laid?

These examples highlight one of the key problems that should be kept in mind in a discussion of the impact of a criminal problem on the criminal justice system, for in any system composed of relatively autonomous subcomponents, the interaction effects within the system can easily be overlooked. If an external factor—a particular criminal problem such as terrorism—acts primarily on one component of the total system—for example, law enforcement in the form of crime prevention—this externally induced pressure affects the internal functioning of the entire system.

The word *system* in the phrase "criminal justice system" implies a high degree of cooperation and well-meshed coordination among the various subsystems that make up the entire system—that is, among the police, courts, corrections, and judiciary. This, however, is not true. As Hulsman points out, "within the system there is a lack of cohesion, there are no common aims, there is considerable role diffusion, there is no coordination between the different subsystems, and there are often differing opinions about roles."[2]

Both the public and the officials within the criminal justice system itself tend to consider the objectives of the individual elements in the system to be contradictory, especially when considering the relation between law enforcement and corrections. In Austin MacCormick's words:

... many citizens as well as law enforcement personnel believe ... that the police catch the offenders, the courts sentence them, the prisons and other

21

correctional institutions then proceed to pamper them, and the parole boards turn them loose on the streets as soon as possible.[3]

As a reflection of this lack of cohesion and uniformity of goals within the criminal justice system, calls for reform are most often addressed to one particular subsystem, with a total disregard for all other connected subsystems. There seems to be an implicit faith that changes in one subsystem will affect just what ailment is being remedied without having any side effects on the partner subsystems.

For example, law-and-order advocates push for increased effectiveness of law enforcement; governmental funds pour into training and updating police departments and law enforcement agencies. One result, of course, is stepped-up surveillance and increases in numbers of arrests and convictions. However, another result, which is perhaps unexpected, at least to the narrow vision of reformists focused on one subsystem instead of the whole system, is a rise in court traffic, backlogs and the resultant "reform" of plea bargaining, and ultimately, more people in correctional institutions. Thus, the side effects for the corrections subsystem are more overcrowding, less manageable populations, and further discontent. Also, if at the law enforcement link, greater effectiveness in apprehension and conviction is limited to certain racial or ethnic or economic groups, inequities in the distribution of inmate populations are exacerbated. In turn, attempts to decrease the influx of offenders into prisons that focus on increased use of probation provide another example of the side effects of narrow reform measures. In this case, law enforcement officers begin to encounter offenders on the street a short time after they arrested them (if the court backlog is not too great), and a feeling of frustration at the law enforcement level is felt. The entire juvenile system, originally a high-minded reform, is another good example of an area where many problems that the criminal justice system faces today stem from previous attempts at reform that focused on a single problem.

Such measures also tend to result in a highly competitive attitude on the part of each component within the criminal justice system rather than a cooperative attitude that is the necessary prerequisite for coordinated, systematic policies and programs. Only when the criminal justice system and all its components are viewed as a coordinated system with common goals can effective methods of crime control be implemented. Thus, in considering the impact of a particular criminal problem (e.g., terrorism) on the operations of the criminal justice system, we must keep in mind not only the more obvious, direct effects of the problem on any one aspect of the system (e.g., law enforcement) but also the indirect effects on all aspects of the system. Every commitment toward one goal affects every other actual or potential commitment of that system.

Consider, for example, the case of law enforcement strategies to control terrorism. Clutterbuck[4] describes the use of a large spy network to monitor underground preparations for potential terrorist acts. This strategy involves the training of personnel. However, the personnel will be useful only as long as there are numerous underground preparations going on; otherwise, they represent a waste of resources. Furthermore, the expenditures involved in the training of the personnel may result in their being used for other purposes than those originally planned. While some purposes may be considered acceptable and admirable, for example, monitoring organized crime networks, other purposes may be questionable in a democratic society, for example, monitoring activities of private citizens in the name of internal security. Thus, a short-sighted, reactive commitment of resources can result in the long run in either a wasteful or abusive utilization of these same resources, all in the cause of justifying their continued use once the situation that triggered the original resource allocation has passed.

Keeping this example in mind, we can raise the question, to what degree do certain current or proposed strategies directed toward combatting terrorism provide a potential source of future problems or problematic side effects? Herein lies an issue where the impact of terrorism on the criminal justice system and the response to it provide intriguing and valuable areas for future research: Will laws specifically tailored to deal with terrorism today become obsolete, or can they be applied in different contexts tomorrow? An example from the skyjacking case might be the potential resolution of the legal question surrounding airport screening procedures. To what extent does military hardware and electronic equipment purchased (and even created) to deal with terrorism via the target-hardening approach divert limited financial resources from other problems? Related to this question is the issue of whether highly specialized and trained personnel are less able to adapt their job effectiveness to fluctuating needs of the system in which they operate.

While we have already mentioned some of the side effects certain sentencing practices can have on various components of the criminal justice system, the issue of sentencing also raises problems within the broader context of the goals of the system as a whole: To what extent does "combatting terrorism" mean preventing or stopping terrorist activity and to what extent does it mean dealing with it as it arises? The implications of each attitude are different. For example, the first interpretation might lead to a policy of deterrence whereby convicted terrorists are severely punished. The second might, on the other hand, lead to a policy whereby terrorists are treated as are all persons convicted of criminal activities of similar import. While this approach might function, among other things, to decrease the "martyrability" of a convicted terrorist, the goal would not be a deterrent one necessarily, but simply one of "normal" disposition of a convicted offender. Thus, sentences mandated for specific terrorist acts can be applied according to how terrorists and their acts are viewed; within the context of the goals of the criminal justice system, there is the practical problem of whether terrorism can be narrowly enough defined to facilitate sentencing procedures uniquely adapted to terrorists and their disposition.

Finally, there is the problem of the extent to which a commitment should be made toward meeting the goals of the system, which raises the question: Is it conceivable that the current commitment to "combatting terrorism" is simply a reflection of the fluctuating intensity of a particular social phenomenon? As pointed out in Chapter 2, Hamblin and Miller[5] have suggested that skyjacking activity has occurred in discrete waves or "epidemics" over the past decades and that deterrent strategies and policy decisions have echoed these waves with synchronous waves of their own. Once the technological and financial commitments were made, the number of incidents of skyjacking diminished precipitously. Only the impetus of an "epidemic" of skyjacking was needed to stimulate an appropriate and commensurate response.

Now, here is the crucial point. In terms of optimal use of societal resources (the criminal justice system and its various elements being part of these resources), a foolish, even detrimental, approach would be to divert too much energy into combatting a fluctuating phenomenon. The commitment of resources to this end (i.e., combatting terrorism) must itself be flexible enough to allow for the fluctuations in the incidence of the phenomenon to be combatted. An example of flexibility was exhibited when the Sky Marshall Plan was dropped after screening procedures began,[6] despite the commitment of time, money, and personnel. While a full-scale commitment to combatting terrorism may be beneficial on a short-term basis, it may not be beneficial on a long-term basis: A commitment to one goal necessarily reduces the availability of certain resources (namely, the subsystems within the criminal justice system) for other pressing social (and criminal) problems.

The above examples of the possible side effects of the criminal justice system response to terrorism make clear that when considering ways to combat terrorism (or any criminal problem), we should always maintain the "systems" perspective—that is, systems within systems within systems that are all delicately balanced and subject to alterations by external impact as well as by the internal impact stemming from those outside influences. When considering the impact of terrorism on the operations of the criminal justice system, we must keep in mind not only the goals of the system but the perhaps at times invisible interdependency of its various subsystems and the interdependency between the criminal justice system as a whole and other institutions within society.

Thus, in studying various aspects of criminal justice handling of terrorism and skyjacking, we should also consider the implications of various tactics and strategies for the social order itself. As noted in Chapter 1, from the perspective of a democracy, the dangers or social costs of combatting terrorism are an integral part of the problem, for the cure may ultimately be worse than the disease—and this is the intent of the terrorist.

One of the stated aims of terrorism, as noted by Clutterbuck[7] is to make everyday life so unbearable and uncertain for the average citizen that the existing public authority will be undermined and the average citizen will at best welcome and support or at least tolerate and sympathize with guerrilla forces. In this view, the terrorist activity ultimately leads to the collapse of the existing authority and a restructuring of society, but, as also noted by Clutterbuck, the most common outcome of terrorist activity is not as stated in its aims. In fact, what usually happens is the establishment of a strict, authoritarian regime involving routine suppression of individual liberties that, ironically, is fully accepted by the average citizen as the price one must pay for day-to-day security and stability.

A fairly recent example of this outcome occurred in response to the Canadian government's invocation of the War Measures Act during the October Crisis of 1970 when the FLQ kidnapped Pierre Laporte and James Cross. Although the War Measures Act gave the police wide-ranging powers, including authority to enter private homes and detain people indefinitely without laying specific charges, few citizens complained and most supported the action, though protest began to mount later on.

The great challenge for modern Western democracies is to combat terrorism without recourse to the suppression of individual liberties that is so prevalent in many countries that have a long history of violent political protest. Interestingly, Dror[8] suggests that the ability to do so constitutes a false hope in the face of constant terrorist threat. In fact, in several countries, including Italy and the United States (California), legislation has been drafted prohibiting the payment of ransom by relatives of hostages or by private groups when the kidnapping has political motives. Such proposals reflect a change in attitude that is consistent with the current Israeli position, which takes a very hard line.

A hard-line type of strategy is only beginning to be considered in European countries, particularly those with a strong humanistic tradition, such as Holland. Here is a concrete example where the dual focus mentioned at the outset can be applied to future research. Holland has had a number of terrorist incidents recently. How have these events, and success or failure of attempts to deal with them, affected the Dutch criminal justice system and its attitudes to crime control and treatment of the offender? Are the lessons being learned in one country applicable to other countries?

Another example of the danger or social cost of combatting terrorism is that the national criminal justice basis for maintaining social order too often leads us to consider terrorism as if it were a kind of war, perhaps a kind of civil war or an urban guerrilla war. If terrorist activity is considered to be an act of war, the criminal justice system may be the inappropriate social institution to deal with it except insofar as it has precedent in dealing with certain aspects of warfare. The relevance of this issue to the main concerns of this discussion is directly proportional to the degree to which the criminal justice system should be involved in combatting surrogate warfare. While in many countries the armed forces and the police forces tend to be synonymous, this tradition is not the accepted one in most Western democracies.

The challenge, then, is not to push the war analogy very far, since it can have misleading, if not indeed dangerous, implications by overdramatizing or distorting the potential threat of terrorism. Such an interpretation has led in some instances to the creation of paramilitary forces that use methods that closely parallel, indeed are sometimes identical to, those used by the terrorists themselves. In terms of the impact of such an approach on the operations of the criminal justice system itself, we might ask to what extent the problem of terrorism is causing the criminal justice system to make financial and personnel commitments to a surrogate warfare definition of the terrorist problem? In terms of the implications for the larger social order, we could ask: How far can we go before the scales tip over? When do we reach the point of no return? Herein lies the dilemma. While no one can deny the effectiveness of war-like counterterrorist tactics, upholding the rule of law and safeguarding the integrity of the criminal justice system is of the utmost importance. We can argue that it is "better to suffer the slings and arrows of outrageous fortune" rather than threaten the delicate balance that the criminal justice system was originally designed to uphold. Conversely, we could argue that this general concern for the sanctity of the law is mere hypocrisy, since such forms of counterterrorism will be exercised "under the table" in any case. Both viewpoints have some validity and could probably be reconciled by acknowledging that this type of counterterrorism is one possible, but not exclusive, solution to the problem. Such patchwork solutions, however, are merely reactive and are based on the assumption that terrorists give up easily or do not have genuine grievances.

Oppenheimer[9] once said that the best way to prevent the rapidly accelerating slide of our global village toward a man-induced Hell was to "let it happen." Could the best approach to combatting terrorism be "let it happen"? What might this actually mean? Let us assume it does *not* mean ceasing the type of preventive strategy typified by the skyjacking case. For a great many people, the effects of terrorism are very unsettling, and clearly, something should be done about it. As demonstrated by the skyjacking case, things *are* being done; laws are being passed; preventive strategies are being implemented; policies are being modified. Yet the terrorism goes on. Perhaps this is unavoidable, and rather than let it happen, we should, as Clutterbuck says, learn how to live with it.

This approach implies that we must stop taking terrorists for granted and begin to ask questions. As long as we focus on traditional, well-tested methods and solutions, we shall continue to be caught in the double bind implicit in the war analogy. As soon as we begin to ask why terrorists act as they do, we are forced to view their actions and our responses to their actions, in terms that can best be described as a kind of communication: As more and more people become aware that terrorism stems from a continuing process of sociopolitical change, then appropriate solutions will be sought in response.

In discussing how the criminal justice system can best cope with the problem of terrorism, we should keep in mind the various problems and issues raised in this analysis of the impact of the response to terrorism by the criminal justice system. The following two chapters will focus more specifically on the possible responses of the different components of the system to the unique problems posed by political terrorism. These include judicial processing and sentencing and institutionalization. In doing so, we shall deal primarily at the national level and concentrate on the workings of any given system of justice.

4 Problems of Judicial Processing and Sentencing

The criminal justice system is a formal societal defensive reaction to intolerable behavior. From the beginning, it was conceived as a tool designed to protect an established order of values attuned to the political organization of the community. Transgression of some important norms reflecting these values was seen as a crime and, as such, demanded punishment. The reasons invoked to justify such punishment changed over time and still engender considerable controversy. However, what is relevant to our analysis is not so much the premises underlying such a tradition of repression but its very application.

Judicial processing and sentencing are activities governed by the rule of law and by the rule of practice. The current problems relating specifically to terrorism in connection with judicial processing and sentencing revolve primarily around the question of achieving the same amount of fair justice in different contexts and in the face of mounting pressures upon the court system. In line with the sequential approach that we have adopted, let us look at these problems and the judicial process in a similar fashion. The elements in the judicial process are threefold: the nature of the court, the procedures of the court, and the sentencing.

As we have seen in earlier chapters, terrorism is being treated more and more as a special criminal problem. This fact is manifest in the evolution of specialized law enforcement units, the use of the military in domestic conflicts, the adaptation of current legislation to changing forms of old crimes, and even the introduction of new laws. The next logical step in this reactive trend would be to consider the possibility of creating a special court to deal with the special problem.

What would a special court entail? While a tempting argument is that special courts would provide the judicial apparatus, personnel, and procedures necessary to deal effectively with a unique problem, the fact also seems inevitable that such a development would also entail a discriminatory approach in terms of the personal orientation and attitude of the judges and maybe even in terms of substantive penal law and criminal procedure. The solution, therefore, is not as neat as it seemed at first glance.

The prohibition of special courts included in both the German (FRG) and Italian constitutions is no coincidence, and we should look closely at the reasons underlying these provisions. Both these countries have had the unlucky experience of living under the totalitarian spirit of nazism and fascism. Under such regimes, special courts appeared under the guise of criminal justice serving the interests of the community. In actual fact, they were political courts operated by biased officials whose ultimate aim was to suppress the recalcitrant opponents of the regime and to make sure that anyone else harboring doubts kept them to themselves.

Such a danger should not be dismissed in the belief that we are immune to similar abuses. The fact that the victims of these abuses have not relied merely on the power of recollection, but have gone as far as to provide legal assurances against potential recurrence, attests to the validity of the threat. Over and above this problem, however, there are other, more technical obstacles to the creation of special courts.

The most obvious of these are: staffing problems, political independence of the judges, criteria for selection of cases, and the polarization of public attitudes. Even though these problems are common to the judicial processing of any crime, they seem to be more acute in the case of political terrorism. This situation stems from the fact that political terrorism casts doubt upon the validity of the system itself instead of simply abusing the system to further personal goals. Most criminal activity uses the system to further legally proscribed ends. Political terrorism works outside the system and challenges it in the process. Thus, it strikes an immediate emotional chord in officials and public alike and tends to be perceived as a uniquely urgent problem that is more threatening than "ordinary" violent crime.

The staffing problem is twofold. On the one hand, one must try and guarantee a minimum level of impartiality, which might be difficult to achieve in view of the emotional response to such cases. On the other hand, there is the distinct possibility that qualified persons may be reluctant to serve on such courts. The resulting public visibility carries attendant dangers that are not paranoid fantasies, as evidenced by the assassination in April 1977 of the Federal Public Prosecutor in West Germany, who was in charge of the prosecution of the Baader-Meinhof group. We can also cite the 1970 incident in San Rafael, California, in which a judge was kidnapped from his courtroom and killed in the ensuing shoot-out with police.

Related to this staffing problem is the temptation to appoint politically biased judges to head these courts. Certainly no one would be surprised if a government chose not to take any chances on the fidelity of the judges. Even if a government takes all possible precautions to ensure the impartiality of the judges, the very act of creating a special court can too easily be used, either by the terrorists or even the press, as proof that the cards are stacked.

Once we have created and staffed a special court, who goes before it? Since, as pointed out in Chapter 1, defining political terrorism is so difficult even in theory, why should it be simpler in practice? Possibly, we could go as far as finding agreement on a very narrow range of cases, since agreement is usually easy to achieve under the pressure of special circumstances. However, what happens when the agreed-upon terrorists have all been tried and the special court runs out of business? The traditional solution, as we have seen in the previous chapter, is to look for new customers in an effort to justify continuing operations and fund allocations. This effort necessarily leads to a broadening of the selection criteria. In view of the special focus of these courts on political terrorism, there is the distinct danger that, once the terror is over, the new criteria will encompass political activities whose terroristic quality is more doubtful. The step that leads to an atmosphere of breeding suspicion and mistrust is not very great.

As well as the problems surrounding the nature and functioning of the special courts themselves, we must also take into account the impact of these courts on public attitudes. We feel that this impact will involve a polarization of concepts, interpretations, and perceptions of political terrorists and their interactions with established authority. The two extremes of such a polarization are, on one hand, the overdramatization of the terrorist threat and, on the other hand, the glorification of terrorist acts.

As should be clear from the above, the easy solutions that special courts seem so readily to provide lead to many more problems than they could possibly solve. Given the rejection of the option of special courts, the next logical step is to look at the court system that we already have. Even though this system has undeniable defects, it may turn out, at least for the time being, to be the best vehicle for judging terrorist acts. While this solution may be obvious, we must analyze the actual procedures in order to see where special difficulties might arise.

The use of ordinary courts does not necessarily imply the use of standard procedures. Just as we can create a special court to deal with a special problem, we can also create new procedures within the existing system. The by now familiar temptation to react with special tools, be they special police units or courts, will certainly not disappear when we choose to confine ourselves to already established judicial structures.

The area where this tendency would be most likely to manifest itself is in the rules of evidence. How does one go about preparing a criminal case against a political terrorist? Traditionally, one relies on the investigatory work of the police and on the testimony of witnesses. Relying on the ordinary citizen to accept the heavy burden of responsibility inherent in testifying is difficult in these cases. The clearest danger for witnesses is the visibility they acquire in light of the atmosphere of intimidation that usually surrounds such cases.

In fact, we should distinguish between three types of witnesses: the victims, the collaborators, and the observers. The victims, because of their experience, are probably scared and want to forget the whole business as quickly as possible. Asking them to prolong the ordeal in a sometimes lengthy and sensational trial may be too much. Thus, this traditional source of evidence is one on which the court can seldom rely in terrorism cases. This situation may also apply to the collaborators, though for different reasons. Such potential witnesses may refuse to testify out of a sense of loyalty to the terrorist cause, or out of fear of retaliation if they turn state's evidence. The observers are the last recourse. The ordinary citizen who happened to see something that could be used by the prosecution may be subject to the same fears as the victim, whether these fears are justified or not. In such situations, the reality of the threat is not what is important, but the belief that it exists, as is true of many cases involving the use of violence. The woman who waited four days before calling the police after she had come face to face with the "Son of Sam" on the night of his last murder in August 1977 is a good example of the effects of fear on potential witnesses. The end result is that the only reliable source of witnesses consists of those observers who were on the scene by virtue of their official duties. In other words, ultimately police officers may be the only witnesses to possess both a knowledge of the facts and the willingness to report them.

Given this primary dependence on the police for eye-witness testimony and given their official monopoly on criminal investigation, we see that the police play a particularly important role—we might even say an inflated role—in cases involving political terrorism. This accumulation of judicial functions understandably leads to considerable pressure. In view of the special challenge posed by the political terrorist, the law enforcement community can easily feel compelled to succeed. Public sentiment, particularly as reflected in sensational, melodramatic media coverage, can exacerbate this attitude and lead to the belief that, in this particular case, there is absolutely no room for failure without the risk of undermining confidence in the authorities, on the part of both the general public and the authorities themselves.

Such emotionally charged situations tend to raise issues of national security and to produce high expectations for effective action and immediate results. Some of the possible dangers that can arise in the process of investigation and preparation of a case include the use of illegal methods for acquiring evidence, the infringement on civil rights, and the tampering with any evidence that is available. Once a case is brought to court, further possible pitfalls include the relaxing of the rules of evidence, the admission of biased testimony, collusion between prosecution and defense, or prejudicial interventions by the presiding judge. We have only to look at past cases where questions of national security and attendant public outcry combined to produce hasty legal decisions that were proved to be highly questionable or even wrong at a later date, once the emotional atmosphere had passed. The Dreyfus case in pre-World War I France, or the Rosenberg case in Cold War-conscious America are two examples. The 1969-1970 conspiracy trial of the Chicago Seven (initially Chicago Eight) also tarnished the image of the judicial process, primarily because the presiding judge allowed himself to be provoked by the inflammatory actions of the defendants.

Closely related to the problems outlined above is the role of the media in feeding the emotional climate that typically surrounds cases of political terrorism. The most obvious effects are those that serve to bias potential jurors, aggravate the natural fears of potential witnesses, and put law enforcement and judicial officials under even greater strain. The media, even though governed by the requirements of profit as are most other institutions, must also accept the undeniable social responsibilities that go hand in hand with the power they are granted. Informing the public is a catch-all principle that can be applied in many ways. However, the resulting public knowledge should be of the type that increases understanding and allows for informed judgments of the facts and issues.

The last step of the judicial process is sentencing. What special problems might arise at this stage? Even though most criminal justice systems seem to treat acts of political terrorism as though they were ordinary crimes, the validity of this assumption can only be tested by analyzing the sentences given to political terrorists as opposed to ordinary criminals. While we might argue that major crimes such as murder, bombing, or kidnapping will show no differences in sentence because they are considered to be very serious no matter what the context or the motive of the offender, the sentencing of minor crimes, such as possession of firearms or illegal use of the telephone or the mails, will reflect differences and thus cast doubt upon the official apolitical position. The danger of treating the political terrorist as a special offender is as present in sentencing as we have seen it was in regard to the courts and their procedures.

The most obvious problematic areas in this context are the nature and length of the sentence and the granting of probation. Because of the atmosphere surrounding cases of political terrorism, longer and stiffer sentences tend to be demanded, and probation is less likely to be granted. Underlying these problems is the dual pressure on the courts (as on the entire criminal justice system) from within and without. On the one hand, the system views itself as ultimate defender of the social order and therefore feels compelled to react forcefully to the terrorist threat. On the other hand, public attitudes, particularly as reflected in the mass media, exert pressure on the courts from the outside. This external pressure tends to force the courts into short-term, reactive responses while, at the same time, it increases the credibility of the court's perception of its role and thus intensifies the internal pressure.

One interesting result of this kind of pressure to act quickly and severely is that long sentences are often handed down in the heat of the controversy, only to be followed at a later date by such practices as pardons, amnesties, or early release on parole once the sense of urgency is gone. These practices minimize the impact of the sentence and illustrate the need to consider adapting the judicial procedures *before* being forced to do so by the usually hysterical climate that surrounds most terrorist cases.

The critical tone of this chapter was a deliberate tactic adopted to expose the very real pitfalls that lie in the path of those who use the criminal justice system to fight political terrorism. We believe that this system is still the only proper tool to deal with the problem and that we must be extremely sensitive to preserving, and when possible, increasing its integrity. We should also point out that some countries do not even bother with the problem of justice and resort either to deportation or summary execution.

5 Problems of Institutionalizing Political Terrorists

Once political terrorists have been tried and convicted, what is done with them? If they are not extradited or deported or executed, they are usually placed in a prison or some other correctional institution. In discussing institutionalization as a means of coping with convicted political terrorists, we should realize that the entire concept of institutionalization or imprisonment is under severe scrutiny and criticism nowadays. Therefore, in the ensuing discussion, we will distinguish between those problems inherent in institutionalization per se and its attendant goals and philosophies, and those problems specifically related to the institutionalization of political terrorists. While some problems posed by political terrorists are applicable to most if not all types of offenders, some problems are unique to political terrorists and perhaps other special categories of offender, such as the violent or the "hard core."

As is generally recognized, the goals of imprisonment are threefold: punishment, incapacitation, and rehabilitation. These goals are not mutually exclusive and can be emphasized in varying degrees in different penal policies. By avoiding a clarification of their positions on the matter, prison administrators tend to believe that they have satisfied everyone, but in fact they are only perpetuating a very ambiguous situation. This ambiguity is exacerbated when the system comes under a great deal of pressure due to unusual events, such as riots, hunger strikes, and so forth, or to the presence of exceptional individuals, such as the politically motivated offender.

In addition to the ambiguity surrounding the goals of imprisonment, each individual goal is liable to certain criticisms and indeed have come under increasing attack in recent years. While one view of punishment involves various types of physical and mental abuse and prisons as the appropriate institutions for carrying these out, there is an increasing trend to consider deprivation of liberty per se as sufficient punishment. Thus, we speak of incarceration *as* punishment as opposed to incarceration *for* punishment. This approach requires us to look more closely at the prison environment with an eye to minimizing those aspects of prison life that are punishing to the offender over and above simple incarceration.

The view of punishment *as* incarceration is fully consistent with the second goal of imprisonment, namely, incapacitation. Here, the objective is simply to remove offenders from the social milieu and to isolate them in a special institution so that they are literally incapable of committing more crimes. The most obvious problem in this case revolves around the length of the sentence.

35

The decision as to when an offender can be allowed to reenter the mainstream of society is a very tricky one. The easiest and "safest" solution is to put off such a decision indefinitely, and this procedure has led to what is now called the indeterminate sentence. One solution that has been increasingly favored is the fixed sentence in which an offender is not eligible for parole for a predetermined time that is specific to a particular crime.

The traditional solution to the problem of when to release offenders is embodied in the third goal of imprisonment—that is, rehabilitation. In this case, the objective is to create changes in the behavior patterns of the offenders so that they will abandon their antisocial ways and will, upon release, integrate into society at large. Thus, we speak now of "correction" or treatment of the offender. This approach is inspired by the medical model whereby offenders are considered sick or at least socially maladjusted and can be cured by appropriate treatment techniques. Criticisms of this model have focused either on the context in which change is attempted or on the justifications for doing so in the first place. The first criticism is leveled at the prison itself, and the solution is seen to lie in the community—hence the concept of community corrections.

The second criticism of the medical model focuses on the idea of treatment itself. On the one hand, as illustrated by the antipsychiatry movement, emphasis is placed on the integrity of individual persons and their right to be different. Furthermore, the point is made that the medical model facilitates and justifies a sometimes abusive use of the indeterminate sentence. On the other hand, there is an increasingly repressive attitude whereby treatment programs are viewed as the coddling or pampering of hard-core criminals. This view leads back to an emphasis on the first goal—that is, punishment.

How do the three goals of imprisonment and their possible interactions apply to the political terrorist? Theoretically, punishment is directed at the act. We judge a person insofar as he has committed a prohibited act, not as a person per se. We sentence the perpetrator, not the person. Even so, the motive behind the act is not forgotten altogether. Traditionally, motives serve as mitigating factors, for instance, in extradition and in sentencing. Of course, motives can be used the other way. The motive behind terrorist acts might be used to demand harsher sentences and to make sure that the perpetrators are properly punished.

Depending on which point of view we take, the convicted terrorist can be considered either as a political prisoner or as a criminal offender. The use of punishment as mere revenge works as well for political terrorists as for any other kind of offender. But punishment is supposed to be more than revenge; it is conceived as a means of deterrence. Even though the deterrent effect of punishment is doubtful in many cases, it appears to be totally inappropriate in the terrorist case. Possible imprisonment, let alone death, is just one of the risks that a terrorist assumes in the name of a particular cause.

In view of the committed terrorist's imperviousness to punishment and deterrence, the goal of incapacitation appears to be more appropriate. A striking fact is that the most visible terrorists tend to be young, and we could cynically suggest that if we keep them off the streets long enough, they will tire of their game. On the other hand, there seems to be evidence that growing older does not guarantee retirement, as illustrated in Northern Ireland, where fathers and sons fight side by side, interrupted occasionally by periods of imprisonment.

The final goal of imprisonment—rehabilitation—is where the motivation of the terrorist is likely to present the most serious obstacles. Given the level of commitment to a cause and given the general inefficacy of most treatment programs, even for the "average" criminal, it is highly doubtful that treatment will change political terrorists. This does not mean that effective change is impossible. The question is are we willing to pay the social cost of enforcing conformity. Let us not forget that, officially, the terrorist has been singled out for what he did and not for what he thinks, and every person should have an inviolable right to perceive and judge his world in any way he wishes.

One form of rehabilitation that can and probably should be made available to all prisoners, including the political terrorist, is education and training programs. However, participation in such programs should never be mandatory, nor should it be a prerequisite for granting parole or other privileges. The status of prisoner of war (POW) appears at first sight to be another possible solution to providing special programs for political prisoners without violating their individual rights. By virtue of his political motivation, the terrorist can be viewed as a POW and, as such, be given special privileges like not wearing a prison uniform, access to the press, or greater opportunity for visitors, such as is the case in France. On the other hand, however, the application of POW status could result in the use of the definition of the prison as the place to carry out special punishment, such as torture, solitary confinement, or segregation in substandard quarters, rather than rehabilitation. Some countries (e.g., the Federal Republic of Germany and the United States) are opposed to the POW approach since they feel that it tends to glorify the terrorist. Thus, the tendency in these countries is to avoid all labels such as POW or "political prisoner" and to view terrorists as "common" criminals. Aside from the issue of glorification, the use of POW status could very easily amount to an indeterminate sentence in cases where the context in which terrorism occurs is a persistent one—as is the case in Northern Ireland.

Whether or not a special status label is assigned to political terrorists, we can legitimately ask whether integration into the prison population or isolation is more likely to serve the interests of rehabilitation. We can hypothesize that political prisoners, like other special types of offenders, represent a potentially disruptive element in the prison community; in fact, in Italy, the prisons constitute one of the primary recruiting grounds for extremist groups. As a result, officials tend to opt for segregation of those prisoners whom they feel are engaging in recruitment activities. Although segregation avoids this problem, others ensue that are detrimental to the goal of rehabilitation. Segregated groups of prisoners who share ideological views or a political cause tend to organize along military lines, to develop hierarchies of command, and to maintain a high degree of internal cohesiveness. The result is an esprit de corps that constitutes an effective barrier that makes movement or communication in either direction extremely difficult, if not impossible. Prison authorities have little control over the activities of individual group members, and, at the same time, those individuals wishing to dissociate themselves from the group are essentially locked in.

Ultimately, any decision to isolate political terrorists should not be based on a policy relating to a specific type of offense, but should be based on the behavior of the individual offender. Any policy of segregation should not be linked to terrorists per se, but should be implemented on an ad hoc basis, according to local needs and circumstances.

In sum, political terrorists do appear to pose some unique problems to correctional institutions because of their political orientation. Any special treatment to remedy these problems or to satisfy the goals of institutionalization is, however, fraught with dangers that range from glorification of the terrorist to institutional violence.

6 The Challenge of Terrorism for the International Community

Until now, we have looked at the problems posed by terrorism primarily at a national level—that is, the problems faced by the criminal justice system of any particular country. However, terrorists are not so considerate as to confine their activities to those areas for which the traditional apparatus has been conceived. Although nationally confined terrorist activity can be forced into fitting within the boundaries of established judicial structures, how do we go about fitting those activities that go beyond national borders into a type of judicial structure that is almost nonexistent—that is, the international one? For example, skyjacking constituted a new form of criminal activity that was eventually dealt with quite easily at the national level by introducing specific legislation and by developing preventive measures at airports. However, determining the course of action in cases involving more than one country proved to be more difficult.

While the possibility of citizens being skyjacked did not seem enough to force governments into action, the possibility of their not being able to take a plane because none were flying had a galvanizing effect on government cooperation. Thus, the threat of strike by the pilots' associations, rather than concerted action within government circles, was instrumental in initiating the planification and implementation of skyjacking prevention and control programs. In general, for economic and political reasons, governments are slow to react to such problems as terrorism, while the direct targets, or other groups who have much to lose—for example airline pilots, diplomats, bank managers, private security agencies, or insurance companies—demand immediate action to reduce the risk of terrorist attacks or to minimize damage resulting from the attacks. On the national level, such groups can develop strategies on their own, even though official cooperation and help is still needed. However, when foreign individuals or organizations, be they governmental or private, become involved in the terrorism, the possibilities for such actions become extremely limited, even inappropriate.

Given this limitation, what forms can a multinational response to terrorism take? Until now, the response has been directed at specific and narrowly defined issues, the clearest example of which has been the elaboration of sectorial treaties or conventions pertaining to the protection of civil aviation and diplomats. These conventions embody the following principles: (1) an obligation to consider the specific act (to which the particular convention is applied) as a "grave breach" requiring imperative legislative intervention from each contracting state; (2) the requirement either to extradite or to prosecute (*aut dedere aut punire*); (3) the necessity to incorporate into each national legislation a competence rule regarding trial; and (4) the need for collaboration in the administration of justice in relevant cases.

While these principles are commendable and can, in theory, be accepted by all nations, such conventions have had a negligible impact. There are many reasons for this state of affairs. First, some countries refuse to sign because of their overt support of given terrorist groups. To sign such a convention would place them in an untenable position. Other countries refuse to sign because they recognize that doing so would place limitations on future diplomatic, political, or economic actions or interventions. Ironically enough, signing these conventions does not even assure adherence to the principles embodied in them. In fact, those countries that do sign are usually those that would apply these principles whether or not a specific convention existed. Thus, we are obviously very far from seeing a body of international laws that is applicable to terrorism per se, partially as a result of the persistent inability on the part of the world community to agree on a definition of what international terrorism is.

The fact that governments, wrongly or not, are guided by their interests rather than by their principles has lead to the current stalemate. Most countries find advantages in terrorist activities of one kind or another. The problem is that there is no unanimity as to where, when, and how these advantages can be utilized. Thus, by agreeing on a universal definition of international terrorism, every country would run the risk of being compelled to apply its legislative consequences indiscriminately and would therefore have to renounce the gains afforded by an opportunistic application of the terrorist label. Furthermore, given an internationally agreed upon definition, countries would then be open to sanctions from the world community if they persisted in utilizing terrorism for political or economic profit. These sanctions could range from diplomatic pressure through economic boycotts and could go as far as military operations.

There is the possibility of creating an international court to supervise the application of international conventions or agreements. Such a judicial body could assume the responsibility, on the one hand, of codifying and applying the sanctions that are usually implemented by one state against another and, on the other hand, of creating a new category of sanctions reflecting the changing international order that presumably is the impetus for the creation of such a court in the first place. We should not lose sight, however, of the dangers and pitfalls inherent in such an approach. Given the unfortunately natural tendency of nations to form opposing factions and coalitions, such a court could very easily turn out to be an instrument for the repression of some groups by others.

While there seems to be a great deal to be done before we can envision a consensus among nations as to when and against whom to take action in the name of combatting international terrorism, the fact remains that there is unrelenting pressure on governments to do something about the international incidents that are becoming a leitmotif in our daily newspapers. This pressure becomes all the more acute for a particular government when these incidents involve its nationals in one way or another. Even though we have no specific answers to the question of an all-inclusive solution, there already exists a certain number of conventions, both bilateral and multilateral, that provide some guidelines on how governments should act when they are caught with alleged international terrorists within their borders.

The most pervasive problem a government faces is that of jurisdiction. Can a well-known terrorist, who has allegedly committed offenses in several countries, be prosecuted in a country in which he has committed no offense? In other words, can one state prosecute on behalf of another state? What are the criteria for deciding to what state an alleged terrorist should be extradited, if several states claim jurisdiction? If, in two independent incidents, a country apprehends two separate terrorists for which two separate governments demand extradition, how can the principle of equal justice be protected if the extraditing country sympathizes with one terrorist's cause and not the other's? Simply by posing such questions, we can see that the jurisdictional issue has many complex ramifications. This complexity can best be illustrated by examining the principle of extradite or prosecute.

From the point of view of the governmental authority, let us imagine that a suspected terrorist is known to be in a particular country. This person could be either a national of that country or a foreigner. In considering what action to take, if any, the first step is to determine who this person is. To do so, the two most important variables that will be taken into account are whether or not the person was actually involved in any way in a specific terrorist act and, if so, where this act took place. Having established the identity and background of the "terrorist," the possible courses of action are numerous: They include doing nothing, covert surveillance (a wait-and-see attitude), registration with the police, expulsion, extradition, prosecution, or even assassination. Table 6-1 depicts some possible decisions for each type of situation. Thus, while the principle of extradite or prosecute seems at first glance to be the only logical course of action in international cases, we see that, in fact, many other options are available.

Despite the greater complexity found in actual practice, the extradite/prosecute principle remains an important tool in the decision process. By itself, the application of this principle necessitates the overcoming of many ambiguities as exemplified by the fact that an exception—the political offense rule—has been incorporated into the original principle. In theory, this exception allows a country to refuse to extradite persons on the grounds that they might be subject to political persecution, while ensuring that, by prosecution in the host country, justice will still be served. In practice, however, the political offense rule has been used to sidestep the obligation to extradite *or* prosecute, which naturally leads to one of the other options listed in Table 6-1. In the context of international terrorism, the end result of this practice is often an implicit

Table 6-1
Most Probable Courses of Action for Authorities in Dealing with International Terrorists

		Commission of Terroristic Act Within the Country	
		No	*Yes*
Commission of Terroristic Act Outside the Country	*No*	nothing done surveillance registration expulsion	prosecution
	Yes	extradite refuse extradition, but prosecute grant asylum expulsion	prosecute and/ or extradite

condoning of the specific terrorist act. To counter such a trend, the Council of Europe has decided to create an exception to the exception by placing specific acts, such as bombing, assassination, kidnapping, and skyjacking, beyond the scope of the political offense rule. The intended effect is to ensure that those acts that are usually associated with terrorism remain extraditable offenses, despite their political character. Ironically, extradition does not always guarantee prosecution. Just as a country can refuse extradition and yet refrain from prosecuting, so a country can demand extradition without intending to prosecute if the demand is met.

Until now, we have discussed the problem of extradition as if only one country, other than that holding the alleged terrorist, is involved. Unfortunately, this approach is too simplistic in view of the increasing complexity of international terrorist incidents. Implicit in this fact, is the multiplicity of parties involved. We are faced with events that involve several countries, be it through their airlines, citizens, embassies, military bases, corporations, and so on. In a similar fashion, there are terrorists who are wanted in many countries because of their involvement in various separate incidents. Thus, the number of demands for extradition of the same terrorist might very well be such as to create difficulties for the holding country: Is the nationality of the terrorist a relevant factor? What criteria can be used for meeting the demands? Can a hierarchy of extraditable offenses be developed? Who can decide whether the bombing of a public place is more serious than the assassination of a diplomat? Furthermore, there are legal technicalities to consider. The 1976 case of Abu Daoud in France, where both Israel and the Federal Republic of Germany requested extradition and France ultimately released him, is a good example of how tricky the legal issues can be. In this particular instance, the Federal Republic's request came too late according to French legislation, while the Israeli request did not fall within the scope laid down in French-Israeli treaty agreements on extradition.

Our analysis of the options open to authorities in the various situations outlined above indicates that most of the special problems terrorism poses for the international community stem directly from its geographical dimension as described in Chapter 1. This suggests the solution of creating an international court that would have jurisdiction over complex international cases. Can we possibly imagine that such an institution could withstand the contradictory demands and needs of a turbulent world community? We leave this as an open question.

7 Key Elements for Future Analysis

In what follows we shall try to outline the most salient points that emerged from the preceding chapters. These could constitute the main elements upon which further reflections and investigations could be based.

The most consistent theme running throughout our analysis is clearly that the criminal justice system must attempt to deal with terrorism in the way it deals with all other crimes of similar import. A direct corollary of this conception is the attitude that terrorists are ordinary people and their goals are often understandable even though their means for achieving them are not.

The nature of terrorism appears, however, to produce a kind of contradictory attitude toward the terrorist. While we can express great concern for respecting the ideological motivations of political terrorists and refrain from any coercive rehabilitation, we have a concomitant concern for dedramatizing terrorist acts and for deglorifying terrorists themselves. This contradictory attitude is a reflection of the criminal justice response to the sociopolitical dimension of terrorism. On the one hand, this dimension can be squarely faced. Then the question of maintaining a balance between respect for motives and treatment of the offender becomes an issue. On the other hand, one can inflate the dangers inherent in the sociopolitical dimension and choose deglorification as the only recourse available for dealing with it. This does not necessarily mean that we cannot, at the same time, face the political implications and try to minimize the glorification of the terrorist and the act. Achieving such an equilibrium constitutes the primary challenge that the sociopolitical dimension of terrorism poses for the criminal justice system.

Governments can and do feel threatened by terrorism, but they are not the only ones. The public at large is not immune to these fears. The threat of terrorism has two basic elements—the political and the physical—and these are shared alike by the governing and the governed. The political threat evokes visions of catastrophe, anarchy and repression that endanger the peaceful continuity of everyday life. The physical threat is more immediate and personal; it shatters the complacency engendered by the impression that "it can't happen here."

Unwittingly or not, the media plays on these fears. Dangers are exaggerated, incidents are melodramatized, prevalence is inflated, and the word *terrorism* is applied indiscriminately. While the media plays a key role in this process, we must also take into account public expectations, preoccupations, and even morbid curiosity. At the same time that the media sends messages to the public, it also serves as spokesman for public sentiment. Thus, it tends to function as an intermediary between the governing and the governed.

The media conveys messages, the public makes demands, and the government feels compelled to act. The public wants to feel protected by its government, and the threat of terrorism turns out to be a test of the capabilities of the authorities. Furthermore, the confidence of the government in the efficacy of its own institutions is challenged. Trust and confidence are maintained as long as the threat is contained. However, the nature of the threat tends to produce intense and urgent requests for immediate action, the responsibility for which lies primarily in the realm of criminal justice operations. The net result can too often be described as a patchwork, spontaneous response to an immediate situation rendered sensational by the public climate. However, such actions usually turn out to be short-lived due to the episodic character of the triggering events. Thus, the criminal justice system is acting like the parent or teacher who seemingly accedes to the vociferous demands of his children or students, only to go his own way later on, when his charges are preoccupied with new and therefore more interesting problems. Of course, such a strategy also has the advantage of maintaining the confidence of the system in its own acts as well as its judgments. Perhaps this is an admirable type of temporal flexibility built into many kinds of social institutions concerned with power and authority.

It is often argued that those in power know better than those not in power, since only when one is in power can one recognize and evaluate the problems involved. While this statement is true insofar as those in power resist the temptation to overreact in any dramatic situation, there is the other side of the coin. Public outcry can also serve as a reminder to officials that overconfidence in their own knowledge and capabilities can turn out, in the end, to be very costly.

As far as public pressure is concerned, the resistance to developing operations uniquely designed to combat terrorism seems well advised. Measures such as counterterrorist squads, special courts, discriminatory sentencing, specialized institutions or units, and whatever else can be devised usually create more problems than they solve, as we have seen in previous chapters.

While analyzing the interaction of the criminal justice system and terrorism, we have tried to compare experiences in different countries. In so doing, we realized that similar problems were encountered by different nations. In some cases, the knowledge gained by the solutions or failures in one country was transferable to other countries. Unfortunately, this does not always work out. Failure of one type of action does not imply that its opposite will be successful. In fact, we have seen that *any* action taken has its attendant problems. Whether convicted terrorists are isolated or integrated with the general prison population, whether special courts are created or the existing court system is used, whether extradition or prosecution is followed, the solution taken seems to create new problems. The idea of "the best approach" is a most dangerous one, as it obscures our thinking and leads us to believe in definitive answers. Thus far, we have found no solution without side effects.

An analysis of political terrorism in terms of communication, power, and accountability leads to a consideration of political democracy and the liberal tradition. From our own cultural perspective, we are committed to nonviolent methods of bringing about political, legal, economic, and social change. What can be done, though, when such methods are unavailable or are perceived as such? As is so often the case, the solution lies in the question asked. Listening is one of the responsibilities of those in power. If this response is not forthcoming, those with genuine or perceived grievances may feel compelled to resort to culturally and legally proscribed means to gain attention.

The implications of this type of "communication" for prevention and control of terrorism are clear. First of all, the increasingly popular tactic of target-hardening, though clearly effective in the short run, cannot be expected to prevent the continuation of terrorist activities as long as no attempt is made to provide legitimate means to redress grievances. Ideologically motivated terrorists will not be stopped by physical obstacles. They will simply turn elsewhere.

Because of the strength of their involvement, political terrorists are not likely to be intimidated by the threat of punishment. Therefore, legal sanctions are relatively ineffective. However, "communication" of another kind on the part of law enforcement and criminal law can be seen to perform three functions with regard to deterrence of terrorists: (1) repression of the offenders themselves; (2) intimidation of sympathizers who might be tempted to give active support to terrorists; and (3) maintaining the confidence of the general public on which they ultimately depend.

There are many terrorist groups in the world today and the effects of their activities are felt over a wide international area. Their influence on world events is exacerbated by the way in which we gather and report news, by the way we keep ourselves informed. Given the unique position and power of the "communication" media in our society, which so highly values freedom of speech, those within the Fourth Estate should take a look at the role they have played in the past and try to evaluate how they can harmonize with the needs of all groups concerned. Changes might involve a more educational role that makes people more aware of the who, what, and why of terrorism and uses the general public's feelings about terrorism to involve them in the operations of the criminal justice system. Thus, while the final solution or best approach to dealing with the problem of terrorism remains a myth, the kind of communication we have described here may well be the key element on which to base future investigations.

**Part II:
The Impact of
Terrorism: Some
Examples of National
Experience**

Introduction to Part II

Throughout the preceding chapters, we have drawn on specific national examples, comparing, contrasting, using them to draw conclusions or to expose trends. To remain faithful to this comparative methodology, it is only logical to focus more intensely on the detailed experiences of individual countries. Each of the following chapters is devoted to a single country and, despite the fact that the sample is small, the potential for a better understanding of the various ways in which terrorism can affect justice systems should not be dismissed. In fact, the countries chosen vary greatly in the dimensions that are thought to be important in regard to terrorism. These include the heritage of colonialism, the degree of power on the international scene, the varying homogeneity of the population, the political stance in the world community, and so forth.

We have left the focus of the subject matter up to the representative of each country chosen, as is reflected in the different forms and perspectives taken in each chapter. Such a decision was guided by the belief that each author was in the best position to decide what were the important elements for analysis and that the uniqueness of national experiences would most readily emerge given this freedom.

The chapters have been grouped in such a way that the amount of direct experience with terrorism or related problems increases with succeeding chapters. Thus, Belgium and Finland, having had negligible experience with specific incidents, come first. We should note, however, that since the time of writing, Finland has experienced (in 1977) a skyjacking originating from the USSR and, under the terms of a local agreement with the Soviets, returned those skyjackers who were apprehended. We cannot assume, therefore, that negligible experience to date means that this will remain so in the future. In fact, both countries have drafted legislation pertaining specifically to terrorism and skyjacking.

The next three chapters deal with France, Sweden, and the United States, all of which have experienced some terrorist-related incidents. The U.S. chapter deals specifically with institutionalization, the French chapter with legislation, and the Swedish chapter with a chronicle of some specific international cases and their implications for government policy. Finally, we have chapters from two countries that have had considerable experience with terrorist activity: the Federal Republic of Germany, with the Baader-Meinhof movement and its offshoots, and Northern Ireland, with its protracted state of near civil war.

The diversity of the following chapters should make clear that no standardization of national experiences has been attempted by the editors. To do so, we would have had to request similar approaches from our authors with a standard breakdown of topics. What follows constitutes an attempt to convey the flavor of national variations in experience with terrorism and its impact on different aspects of national and international criminal justice. A more systematized approach remains one of the more pressing needs for the future and constitutes a major challenge to the international community.

8 Prevention, Legislation, and Research Pertaining to Terrorism in Belgium

Bart de Schutter

The experiences of Belgium in the area of terrorism are very limited, even close to the zero level. There is almost no "practice," case law, or even much open concern. This situation can probably be understood in the light of the following elements:

1. The relatively small role of Belgium in the international political scene (unlike that of the "hot spots" or the major powers like France and the United States);
2. The relative neutrality of its official attitudes (unlike the Dutch position on the Middle East situation);
3. The effective and serious preventive policing (unlike the more liberal societies of the permissive type, such as The Netherlands, France, or Denmark, where presence in the territory to prepare terrorist actions is easier in the absence of repressive control), which includes protection of embassies, premises of international organizations, airports, and so forth;
4. The absence of "political heritage" situations with tensions or conflict potential (e.g., the recent Dutch cases);
5. The standard of living issue: We all have something to lose.

Measures have been taken to cope with the phenomenon: Instructions have been issued, a bluebook on antiterrorist action exists under the responsibility of the Ministry of the Interior, as well as Sabena regulations for the protection of Belgian airports and aircraft. Since these documents are of a fully restricted nature and could not be obtained, minimum information is included in the following pages.

Sabena Security Measures

Comparable to other airlines, Sabena possesses a full-scale security program against hijacking and sabotage of aircraft. It includes:

1. Predeparture screening on scheduled passenger flights and charter flights: All passengers are electronically screened by hand scanners or walk-through devices (if not available, at least a consent search—including VIP's—by a law

enforcement officer is made; hand articles are inspected by X-ray or hand scanner; and even VIP or diplomatic luggage may be inspected.

2. Aircraft security is provided for unattended planes as well as attended planes.
3. Checked baggage: Special measures (X-ray, decompression chambers, and so forth) are used on high-risk flights or threatened flights.
4. Cargo and mail is inspected.

In addition, other special measures are taken for high-risk flights, and as should also be mentioned, Sabena has refused to allow armed guards to be present aboard planes. Priority goes to safety for all passengers, if necessary, by accepting the terms of the hijackers. Clear and precise instructions are also given for cases of bomb threat.

The protection of the Airport in Zaventem is entrusted to the Belgian police authorities (*gendarmerie*), with the help of Sabena security agents. The protection of the premises is in the hands of paratroopers who patrol on a regular basis. Belgian airports and airlines have been quite safe so far.

Belgian Extradition Practice

There are few cases and limited information. Extradition is a decision to be made by the executive, upon advisory opinion given by the *Chambre des mises en accusation*. This advice is not considered a contradictory judicial decision and, as such, gives no right to an appeal before the *Cour de Cassation*. These advisory opinions are published exceptionally, and access to the files of the ministry is difficult, if not impossible.

Legislation and Practice

The law of October 1, 1833, on extradition contains the principles of nonextradition for political crimes and of nondiscrimination between political refugees. Starting with the French-Belgian treaty of November 22, 1834, all extradition treaties have included the nonextradition clause for political offenders. No definition was given in the treaty, but it included specific and mixed political crimes. The law of March 22, 1856, contains the "Belgian clause" restricting the nonextradition principle and excluding violations against the physical integrity of the head of state or his family. This law was linked to exceptional circumstances and is much disputed now. Some anarchists have been extradited (1883: Cyvocat, anarchist extradited to France), while others have not (1909 to 1923: several refusals concerning Russian anarchists; Italian political crimes labeled as being anarchist). Since the beginning of the twentieth century, the notion of political crime has been interpreted very broadly (1928: refusal to France of Bartholomei's extradition; 1936: to Italy of Bassatini). However, it is worthwhile to note that in many cases the judiciary gave a positive answer to the request. The final decision of the government clearly takes into account the circumstances of political unrest and the risk of a political conflict situation.

A less liberal period occurred during the Franco-Algerian conflict when many disguised extraditions took place through arrests on Belgian territory and release at the French-Belgian border. This practice was possible because expulsion is an administrative measure, without intervention of the judiciary. Upon the intervention of the Minister of Justice, an end was put to this practice (e.g., refusals of extradition to Switzerland of Abarca in 1965 or of FLN-Algerians in 1960).

The latest practice seems to confirm that the question of extradition remains the schizophrenic area of international criminal law; all depends on value judgments. For example, in 1972, Italy received the extradition of three terrorists, but in 1968, Belgium refused to extradite three terrorists to Portugal. There is no obligation to extradite in cases where there is clear violation of basic humanitarian rules.

Legislative Measures

Belgium ratified the Hague Convention of 1970 and signed the 1971 Montreal Convention, as well as the convention on the protection of diplomatic agents of 1973. Implementing penal legislation on the civil aviation issue and a new law concerning the taking of hostages are the only specific legislative activities in direct relation to terrorism.

There is no special provision under Belgian law dealing with terrorism as such. The penal code contains, of course, a number of articles that may be invoked, such as homicide, violations against physical integrity, destruction of property, and so forth.

The law of August 6, 1973, modifies the legislation on *civil aviation* and on *extradition.*[1] Its aim is threefold:

1. To harshen the penalties for acts of sabotage against planes;
2. To create a new crime—the illicit seizure of an aircraft;
3. To complete the extradition law by including acts of sabotage of aircraft as an extraditable offense.

Penalties for a simple act of sabotage lie between five and ten years of deprivation of liberty. Ten to twenty years can be given in cases of inflicting permanent incapacity or permanent illness or in those resulting in the destruction of the aircraft, and lifetime sentence can be applied in cases where death occurred. The law also provides for the right of search of passengers and baggage.

The law of July 2, 1975, concerning holdups and the taking of *hostages*[2] creates a title VIbis in the penal code on the taking of hostages. The penalty provided for is lifetime imprisonment. It can be reduced to fifteen to twenty years in cases of freely decided release of the hostage within five days. The death penalty can be awarded in cases of inflicting death, permanent illness or incapacity, or use of physical torture.

Letter bombs fall under a royal decree of September 23, 1958 (Article 70) on explosives, which prohibits the use of mailing devices for explosive materials. Penalties are fifteen days up to two years of imprisonment and fines ranging between 4,000 B.F. up to 40,000 B.F. Equally applicable is a law of May 28, 1958, on explosives, when used to commit crimes against persons or property (five to ten years; 4,000 B.F. up to 160,000 B.F.) or misdemeanors (one month to three years; 400 to 80,000 B.F.).

Cases Involving Belgium

The following are the cases in which Belgium was involved in one way or another:

September 8, 1969: Attack on the El-Al office in Brussels by three persons, two of whom escaped and one of whom was arrested and handed over to the Libyan Embassy.

May 8, 1972: Hijack in flight of a Sabena plane that landed in Lod where all passengers were released. The four hijackers were PLO members, two of whom were killed by security guards and two of whom are serving life sentences in Israel.

March 1, 1973: Murder of the American ambassador and the Belgian chargé d'affaires in Khartoum (Sudan). Eight PLO members were arrested and sentenced to life imprisonment. The sentence was commuted to seven years, and the hijackers were handed over to the PLO and then held in Egypt. They were finally liberated after the BEA hijack of November 1974 from Dubai to Tunis.

Early 1975: Kidnapping and hostage taking of children by persons of Italian nationality. Extradition was received from Italy, and court action is pending.

October 1975: Belgian consulate in Tripoli taken hostage. The case was nonpolitical in character, and the hostage-taker was arrested by local authorities.

A limited number of bomb or hijack threats were received by Belgian authorities, but no serious cases grew out of them.

State Security Action

As in many other countries (e.g., The Netherlands), a bluebook on terrorism has been established under the responsibility of the Ministry of the Interior. Because of the restricted character of the topic, no fundamental information could be obtained nor access to a copy of the document be had. The center of responsibility lies in the Interior Department, with the support of the Ministry of Justice, the Defense Department and the Prime Minister's Cabinet. If necessary (international cases), the Foreign Affairs Department will participate, as will the Communications Department (e.g., in cases of hijacking). A special trained unit of the police forces (*gendarmerie*) is on permanent standby.

Academic Research

The problem of international terrorism has received only limited attention in Belgian academic spheres. The main publications concentrate around the same research units (e.g., the International Criminal Law Center of the Free University of Brussels). Important dates include:

> *March 19 and 20, 1973:* Conference on *Réflexions sur la définition et la répression du terrorisme* (*Centre de droit international*) with contributions on the undefinable act of terrorism (P. Mertens), new forms of revolutionary combat—the guerrilla problem (Mme. Pierson-Mathy), international terrorism (E. David), the U.N. action (W. De Pauw and E. Suy), extradition issues (Mme. R. Cochard), comparative notions on terrorism (P. Legros), and mechanisms to repress terrorism (B. de Schutter);

> *May 20 and 21, 1974:* Colloquium entitled "Belgium and International Criminal Law" (*Centrum voor Internationaal Strafrecht*), which included a session on terrorism (A. Beirlaen);

> *May 15, 1976:* The Flemish Bar Association, at its bi-annual conference, devoted a full-day session to international terrorism and Belgian legislation (B. de Schutter and R. D'Haenens).

Individual contributions of Belgian scholars to international meetings or conferences have not been listed here, but they apparently center around the same authors (Salmon, Mertens, Beirlaen, and de Schutter). Student papers and nonacademic conferences are not taken into account.

Personal Concern

The main emphasis of my personal interest has been on problems of repressive machineries and issues of jurisdiction. Existence of substantive norms is one thing, effective implementation another. Considering that we are facing an antisocial behavior of an universal nature (a *hostis humani generi*) repression should not be limited to national mechanisms.

Even though the matter of the creation of an international criminal court may be picked up again in the U.N. context, after the agreement reached on the definition of *aggression,* the feasibility of such a court is still not a short-term one. Nevertheless, it is my belief that combined efforts should take place to revive the interest in this court, but one using a different approach—that is, from the mini-crimes on to (eventually) the maxi's; from the individual cases of universal concern (e.g., terrorism) to the (all too hypothetical) state crimes. The crime of aggression would be the end of the line, not the start. Attention should be paid to other possible functions attributable to such an institution besides that of the jurisdiction of trial. Analysis should be made of:

The inquiry system, in the style of a fact-finding mechanism, to be used in the frame of out-of-court settlement;[3]

The possibility of including a law-finding function, where the international court gives a binding interpretation in ruling on an issue of interpretation of an international norm.[4]

Compliance through national courts is the main possibility for the time being. Many countries have sufficient domestic legislation, and a minimum set of international rules exists. New forms should receive a quick international response. Model legislations or attempts for harmonization should not be excluded.

More important is the issue on jurisdiction to prosecute. No theoretical obstacles can be found under international criminal law. Nevertheless, in reality, many countries do not include—or do not yet include—the *universality principle* in their rules on extraterritorial jurisdiction. The argument is that the inclusion of this principle on a more general basis gives more flexibility to extradite or punish (*dedere aut punire*). In the absence of jurisdiction, asylum means no punishment; the only way to avoid this is extradition and that may not be in conformity with our notions of nonextradition of political offenders.

Attention has also been paid to prospective changes in this pattern, called the *process of internationalization of national jurisdiction.* Pleas have been made for:

Special domestic courts (or special chambers) with specialized judges on international crimes;

International *governmental* legal observers in international cases in domestic courts (a system of Permanent Court of Arbitration) who would function as the watchdogs of international criminal law and minimum standard rules of human rights, nature, and so forth;

Mixed tribunals, completed with "international" judges, who would serve in domestic courts (which arrangement is close to a specific international criminal court).

In future studies, these elements may be worked out in detail.

9 Finland: A Country with No Terrorism or Skyjacking

Inkeri Anttila

When asked to give a written account of the experiences my country has had with terrorism and skyjacking, I am in a difficult position. I come from a country that has not seen a single skyjack or even a skyjack attempt, and all we know of terrorist acts comes to us through the horror stories sent by television and the press from abroad.[a]

Thus, I cannot say anything on how the control system has actually functioned, and there is also very little to relate to public discussions and proposals. I can, however, present some conjectures on why Finland has so far been spared from terrorist acts, in the hope that the views I present can possibly shed some light on the question of why these events take place in other countries.

Why Have There Been No Terrorist Acts in Finland?

The views I shall present in this connection are, of course, totally based on speculation. The relative importance of the factors I shall present is something that I cannot verify at all. I shall give a list of these factors in the hope that it will give rise to discussion.

Finland's geopolitical position is significant. Finland is a small country in an isolated position. In the east and the south it borders on the Soviet Union; in the west, beyond a gulf, lies Sweden; and in the north it borders on Norway, Sweden, and the Soviet Union. International traffic through Finland takes place principally from Sweden to the Soviet Union and back. It is obvious that in comparison with, for example, Germany or Italy, a much smaller number of non-Scandinavians travel in Finland on business and pleasure trips; furthermore, they are not even asked for proof of identity. Non-Scandinavians, of course, must present their passports on entering and leaving the country. The free travel zone does not extend into the Soviet Union, where passport control is very strict.

There are hardly any so-called migrant workers in Finland. In this respect, Finland differs from almost every other industrialized country of Western Europe. It is difficult for foreigners to get work permits, and there is little

---

[a]In July 1977, a Soviet plane was skyjacked and landed in Helsinki, but no skyjackings have originated within Finland—Eds.

flexibility in the formal procedure to obtain them. Naturally, the Ministry of the Interior may deport undesirable aliens, and the ministry uses this right.

The major language of Finland, Finnish, is the language of a small area. Finnish is not used in any other country. The languages most like it differ so much that even knowledge of these languages does not directly enable one to understand Finnish. This means that in practice it is very difficult for a foreigner to come to Finland and, for example, find a job unless he first goes to the trouble of learning the language of the country. It is also impossible for a foreigner to hide the fact that he is not a Finn.

Finland has no political prisoners at all in the proper sense of the term. According to the police statistics, not one single case of treason has been reported, at least during the five years from 1970 to 1974. Also, at least during the postwar period, there has not been a single assassination or political murder.

Due to the racial homogeneity of Finland, there is no racial conflict. While it is true that there are a few thousand gypsies in Finland and the courts have dealt with a couple of cases where a merchant has been accused on the basis of the 1970 law on discrimination against gypsies, all in all, the problem of racial conflict has little significance in the country. Finland is also homogeneous in connection with *religion.* Over 90 percent of the population is Evangelical Lutheran.

A small country such as Finland has little political influence. It does not seem very sensible to think that, for example, political minorities in some far-off country would think that they could benefit by kidnapping a Finnish politician or, in general, by demanding that the Finnish government undertake certain measures. Also, if a terrorist act is only intended to attract attention, it would understandably be more attractive to have the act occur in a spot that is politically more important than Finland.

The result of these surmises is that terrorist acts, including skyjacks, should take place principally in countries where:

The country is centrally located, there are many foreigners, and it is on important communications routes;

A commonly used language is spoken in the country;

The country harbors political conflict or its position in international politics is especially important.

The Application of General Crime Control Principles
in Combatting Terrorism

Since terrorism is a form of deviant behavior, one could attempt to analyze how the principles of crime control can be applied to this offense category. Measures of crime control can be divided in, for example, the following manner:

Changing the definition of offenses;

Affecting the motivation of offenders or potential offenders;

Decreasing the opportunity for crime.

Of the categories mentioned, only the second, affecting motivation, belongs to "traditional" crime control policy. In the new mode of thought, however, there are no reasons to concentrate solely on measures belonging to this group.

Changing the Definition of Offenses

Changing the definition of offenses starts from the point of view that it is the law that establishes offenses. Therefore, the law can have a determining effect on the level of criminality if new forms of behavior are criminalized or old ones are decriminalized.

In connection with terrorism, this procedure does not in principle enter the question; the general danger of these offenses sets insurmountable barriers. However, there is reason to mention that under certain conditions terrorism may approach the point of civil war, where in practice the acts perpetrated by the winning side are actually decriminalized or depenalized. Thus, the majority of the area's population or the part of the population that has gained power through these means has in a way "accepted" terrorism and, sociologically speaking, has "redefined" the offense involved.

Affecting the Motivation of Offenders or Potential Offenders

Affecting the motivation of offenders or potential offenders in connection with terrorism, as with all types of crime, occurs in principle either through special prevention or general deterrence.

Lately, the effectiveness of *special preventive measures* has been generally doubted in criminal policy, particularly when speaking of "treatment" that could be accomplished through penal sanctions. However, special deterrence measures also include the "warning effect" as well as the effect of rendering the offender harmless.

It is clear that terrorists are especially poorly receptive to the possible (generally small) curative effect of punishment. In the same way, it is to be supposed that the conditions in modern prisons do not serve to give a convicted terrorist the warning needed to prevent him, once he has served his term, from perpetrating further acts of terrorism. We are left only with the possibility of rendering the offender harmless. This can in principle take place by interning the offender in question in a closed institution for life or at least until he has clearly passed the age group in which terrorists usually fall. In those countries where it is legally possible to use capital punishment, this is one way of rendering the offender harmless.

Are there measures that would have a *general deterrent* effect on potential terrorists? The old way, using as severe sanctions as possible, does not seem to be effective, due naturally to the fact that the certainty of becoming the object of control measures or of having to serve a sentence fully is not very large at present. There can be no doubt that terrorism is a branch of criminality where the significance of the size of the risk of being caught and the risk of having to serve a sentence is decisive.

In this regard, international cooperation is absolutely necessary. Those terrorist acts that are or can be disguised as being political are essentially linked to the possibility that the offenders will seek sanctuary in a state that is prepared to provide them with a safe haven. Only good cooperation based on international agreements can bring about improvement in this respect. One idea that has often been presented is the establishment of an international court to deal with, among other things, these offenders. The Swedish professor Sundberg, for example, has dealt with this idea in several articles. In my opinion, serious thought should be given to the possibilities of realizing this proposal.

Thus, in the traditional criminal policy way of thinking, only two possibilities exist:

Increase the sanctions that render the offender harmless, or in other words, enforce capital punishment and life (long-term) incarceration;

Increase the risk of being caught and the certainty of being punished through international cooperation.

All over the world, terrorist acts are interesting material for the mass media. However, it is very probable that publication of such cases—especially the emphasis on the dramatic side of the story that is often to be found—can be more of a hindrance than a help in controlling terrorism. In the offenses perpetrated by political minorities, one of their apparently essential goals is arousing public attention; in fact, there have been cases where the only apparent motive seems to be to get as much publicity as possible. Even in connection with "ordinary" skyjacks for private gain, and not for political reasons, the limelight of publicity may lead to new attempts. All in all, then, publicity should be lessened and dramatic aspects should be played down. If the case is publicized, the general public should also be equally well informed of the capture of the offenders and of their sentencing. Realization of this principle should only be effected through voluntary measures carried out by the media. Even though difficulties would be encountered in practice, acceptance of it even as a general principle could possibly have some effect on public opinion.

Reduction of the Opportunity for Crime

Reduction of the opportunity for crime, a measure that previously was often considered as being outside the scope of traditional criminal policy, has been the object of increasing attention over the past few years. It has been noted that it may be much simpler, and also much cheaper, to direct resources to the decrease of the opportunity for crime, instead of limiting control measures to the old criminal policy way of thinking. It is easier to prevent offenses than to repair the damages they have caused, and it is easier, for example, to change the behavior of the potential victim than it is to change the behavior of the potential offender.

In regard to terrorism this statement is especially true. Of course, decreasing the opportunities is not simple in all situations. It is almost impossible to prevent someone from placing a bomb in a public place; on the other hand, it may be possible to use efficient technical equipment to prevent an airplane passenger from carrying a bomb or weapon onboard. The airlines of the world can undoubtedly tell us quite a bit about measures along these lines. Naturally, technical safeguards involve important care and costs, and some safeguards require so much that they are impossible to use in practice, at least in connection with air traffic that is supposed to operate swiftly.

Some precautionary measures may also easily give the impression of having gone too far. An example of this can be taken from the European Security Conference held in Helsinki. When the thousand or so delegates to the conference were invited to a garden party at a seaside restaurant, quite a number of precautionary measures were taken; for example, there were so many policemen on the streets that it was difficult even for governmental cars to find a way through the barriers. The coast guard was especially worried about the situation fronting the beach, and they had reason to be: While Gerald Ford, Leonid Brezhnev, Pierre Trudeau, Harold Wilson, and Olof Palme were wandering about on the lawn and sampling strawberries in the twilight, the coast guard saw a boat approaching without the required lights. When the boat did not react to their light signals, the coast guard opened fire, and the two drunken men on the boat were drowned. Under normal circumstances, of course, these deaths would not have happened, as the coast guard would not have fired at the boat. At the time, however, they were especially worried about the possible danger to the guests at the restaurant. Thus, when one is estimating the costs of preventive measures, one factor that must be included is the possible costs of excessive precaution.

10 Terrorist Incidents and Legislation in France

Jacques Léauté

Forms of Terrorism Presently found in France

A distinction has to be made between *domestic terrorism,* through the use of bombs, explosion, fires, and so forth, and *foreign terrorism* in France or within French embassies abroad, primarily involving hostages and bombs.

Domestic Terrorism

In 1974, the French police encountered 173 cases of bomb explosions for political, social, or economic motives. Among these, 136 were related, according to police, to *independence movements* (21 in Britanny, 114 in Corsica, and 1 in the Roussillon); 20 to foreign international terrorist movements; and 17 to other organizations or individuals. The total of the same sort of cases was 139 in 1973. Statistics dealing with domestic terrorism in 1975 have not yet been published,[a] although there seems to have been a strong increase. During a serious riot in August, in Aleria, Corsica, hostages were taken, and two *gendarmes* and at least one civilian were killed. A private wine enterprise, owned by a former French Algerian, was destroyed by fire. During the same month, many other fires and bombings of buildings took place. In Britanny, the main television antenna was destroyed by an explosion and part of the province was deprived of broadcasts. The Palais de Justice of St. Brieuc was partly destroyed. Other destruction also occurred.

Since 1969 (the starting point of the present statistics), there has been one domestic terrorist *skyjacking*: On October 18, 1973, Mrs. Craven was killed by police while attempting, by skyjacking, to compel French authorities to intervene in the Israeli-Arabic conflict. There has also been one case of an *hostage being taken* by terrorists: On March 8, 1972, leftists captured Mr. Nogrette of the Renault Company. The absence of political hostage taking has to be noted in contrast with nonpolitical criminality, where kidnappings of children and adults were rather frequent.

Foreign Terrorism

Foreign international terrorist groups elected France or French embassies as one field of their activities in the following types of cases.

---

[a]At the time of the writing of this article—Eds.

Hostages for political motivations. French police have not issued detailed statistics about hostages being taken for political motivations. However, there is no doubt that between 1970 and 1975 two cases taking place in French embassies abroad were purely terroristic: the capture of the French ambassador in Cuba (October 17, 1973) and the capture of the French ambassador in the Hague (September 13, 1974). There was also the case of the French ambassador in Somalia (March 1975), and on February 4, 1976, 31 children, aged 5 to 13, most of whom were children of French soldiers, were kidnapped in Djibouti while in a bus bringing them to school. A French specialist, Mr. Montreuil, writes in *La Revue de la Police Nationale,* 1974, p. 22, that the figures for hostage taking of an undoubtedly political nature were the following: 1970, 2; 1971, 5; 1972, 2; and 1973 (first half), 2. He does not make a distinction between domestic and international terrorism.

Skyjacking. At Orly Airport in 1971, a Frenchman attempted to skyjack a foreign plane with the prospect of compelling French authorities to send medical support to Bangladesh. Mr. Montreuil lists two cases in the statistics for 1973. One of these, the case of Mrs. Craven, was presented here in the section on domestic terrorism.

There were no cases in 1974. In 1975, a terrorist group attempted to destroy an Israeli airplane with a bazooka. When French police reacted, the group took hostages inside the rest rooms of Orly Airport. One week later, there was a second attempt.

Bomb explosions for terrorist purposes. These have been officially recorded for 1974 only. During that year, 20 bomb explosions were recorded. In 1975, terrorist members of the independent Basque Movement in Spain (E.T.A.) engaged in bombing activities in France.

Murders. Some murders were committed against members of foreign secret services or terrorist organizations. In 1974, one military attaché from the Uruguay Embassy was killed; in 1975, one from the Spanish Embassy. French policemen were killed in Paris in 1975 while trying to capture the famous terrorist "Carlos."

Let us also mention the fact that some French citizens were taken as hostages abroad by dissident foreign groups (e.g., Mme. Claustre in Tchad). French legal competence does not apply in such cases.

Forms of Political but Nonterrorist Delinquency in France

There have been no important forms of pure political delinquency (plots, riots, and so forth) during the last six years. Some offenders who committed robberies or other forms of theft have argued that their motivation was political. They claimed either that they were in need of subsidies for their organizations or that they were compelled to commit the offenses by the capitalist structures of the country. Forms of vandalism, linked to the same order of motivations, occurred as well.

Recently, the attempt to create soldiers' trade unions within the army has led to the arrest of some persons, charged under Article 84 of the Penal Code, which prohibits any activity that could result in endangering national security by demoralizing the armed forces.

The Positive Law Relating to Terrorism

Articles 86 through 100 of the French Penal Code, as modified by the ordinance of June 4, 1960, deal with all aspects of major political delinquency. Articles 86 through 92 deal with attempts, plots, and other infractions against the authority of the state and the integrity of national territory. These include armed revolt and taking over of the armed forces.

The use of bombs is punishable under Article 435 of the Penal Code.

Violent group action against persons and properties has been more severely punished since 1970 through the new Article 314 of the Penal Code.

Taking of hostages is punishable under Articles 341 through 344 of the Penal Code. Article 343 has created a special new offense. Article 343 can be used in cases of terrorist action as well as in cases of nonterrorist and nonpolitical motivation. The court in charge of judging the former case is the *Cour de Sûreté de l'Etat* (see the section below on criminal proceedings).

Skyjacking is a new offense created by Article 462. After the attempt of skyjacking of 1971 (reported in the section on foreign terrorism), where the attempt took place before the taking off of the plane, an addition was made to Article 462 in order to include attempts of skyjacking under the particular crime of skyjacking. Law no. 75-624 of July 11th, 1975, was added, due to the fact that some cases of false reports about skyjacking occurred. Article 462-1 states that communication of false information concerning the security of an airplane in flight will be punishable by imprisonment of one to five years and a fine of 2,000 to 40,000 francs.

Separatist action is punished by Article 88 of the Penal Code already mentioned above. Separatist movements can be charged under this text.

Criminal Proceedings

In former times, French military courts had competence for the judgment of soldiers and even civilians charged with an attempt against external security of the state (*atteinte à la Sûreté extérieure de l'Etat*). The Algerian conflict, having led to the Evian Agreements in 1962, showed how difficult it was to submit highly politically motivated offenses to military courts. After the unsuccessful attempt to create high military courts, a new *Cour de Sûreté de l'Etat* was created in 1963 to specialize in the judgment of, on the one hand, purely political offenses and, on the other, ordinary offenses with special political motivation, as appear in Article 698 of the Penal Code.

Point c of Article 698 is of special interest here because it shows how political motivation withdraws competence from ordinary courts and gives it to the *Cour de Sûreté de l'Etat.*

Law no. 75-624 of July 11, 1975, extends French competence to offenses committed abroad, against personnel of French embassies and consulates, and against French diplomatic and consular buildings abroad.

11 The Antiterrorist Legislation in Sweden

Jacob Sundberg

The Socialist Country

Sweden is often referred to as a neutral and nonsocialist state. These descriptions do not convey much understanding, either of actual facts or why the antiterrorist legislation of the 1970s caused such political turmoil in Sweden.

First of all, the Social Democrats have been in power in Sweden almost uninterruptedly for about half a century, most of the time without any serious challenge.[a] As a result, the bureaucracy and business at large have grown accustomed to this seemingly permanent power structure and have become more or less integrated with the ruling party. As a one-party state in this sense, Sweden shares much of the attitudes of the other socialist states to the south and the east, since the basic, more or less Marxist-oriented analysis of life, society, and power is essentially the same. Indeed, the Swedish government, in the 1950s, openly proclaimed that it was pursuing the same goals as the socialistic regimes in what later came to be known as the "socialist camp."[1]

It is a curious twist to the development that the ruling regime in Sweden domestically refers to itself as socialist and propagates socialism and socialistic solutions, while abroad, in particular in the U.N. context, the "socialist" label has been usurped by the socialist camp states to designate their ideology and solutions. Internationally, thus, Sweden is a "nonsocialist" state, but domestically it is a socialist one. The basic difference between the socialist regimes in the socialist camp and the socialist regime in Sweden boils down to the one that a society's advance into the predetermined stage of "socialism" and eventually "communism" is theoretically reversible in Sweden—due to the acceptance of the possibility that the people in democratic elections may legitimately decide against it[b]—while in the socialist camp the same advance is axiomatically irreversible. Failing any serious challenge to the rule of the socialists, the difference has no practical effect.

The advent of the new states to the United Nations in the early 1960s brought forth a number of U.N. resolutions against colonialism. The Swedish government found in these resolutions ground for financially assisting various liberation movements, particularly those active on Portuguese territory. A reorientation of Swedish foreign policy took place so that a policy of confronta-

---

[a]This article was written before the fall 1976 elections in which Palme's Social Democrat government was defeated—Eds.

[b]As actually happened in the fall of 1976—Eds.

71

tion gradually succeeded the neutral and more prudent policy of the 1950s. The Greek coup of August 21, 1967, particularly incensed leading socialist circles and released a new wave of confrontation. Attempts were made to cultivate the birth of a Greek resistance movement partially directed by the dethroned Greek politician, Andreas Papandreou. He was invited to direct his fight against the Greek regime from Sweden. He cooperated with Brillakis, head of the Greek Communist party, to establish terrorist activity in Greece.

The Swedish attitude towards political refugees developed parallel to this evolution. In the early postwar period it became accepted in Sweden, as in other West European countries, that it was the totalitarian society itself in the socialist camp that made the escape therefrom a political act.[2] These refugees "generally ... had not been politically active in their home countries" but rather had resented and rejected the totalitarian politicization of life that follows from the implementation of socialist dogmas.[3] Escape was thus accepted as a political offense that prevented extradition to the home state, and the practice developed in Sweden, parallel to the simultaneous West European development, to give political refugee status almost automatically to refugees from the Democratic Republic of Germany (DDR) and Poland.[4]

The new confrontation policy made the Swedish government abandon its previous demands that refugees who had been given asylum in Sweden should refrain from political activity in that country.[5] Instead, it was insisted that foreigners should enjoy the same freedom as the Swedes to engage in political activities in Sweden.[6] Since they were not allowed to participate in the Swedish elections, the formula mainly operated to allow the Papandreou type of political activity. The change in attitude—hereinafter referred to as the "Papandreou line"—of course, did not much affect the new arrivals resisting the totalitarian politicization in the socialist camp. What it did, however, was to attract refugees from outside of that camp. According to the commission that was charged with revising the legislation on aliens, a person was considered entitled to political refugee privileges if "he has left out of political reasons ... and it may be assumed that due thereto he will be hit harder."[7] The illegal leaving of a country under dictatorship but without totalitarian features was previously not, as such, a political act. This confrontation policy, however, gave Sweden the reputation as a haven for those elements of political disloyalty that would attract a more severe sentence in the home country of the refugee, if prosecuted there after extradition. Consequently, Sweden turned into a haven for an ever-increasing flow of people who, by pursuing various socialist policies, had attracted the repression of some local dictatorship.

In the 1960s, too, a changing of guards occurred in the Swedish socialist leadership. Two new personalities took the lead. One was the new prime minister, Olof Palme. Named after an uncle who was killed by communists in 1918 in the Finnish civil war in which he had volunteered on the side of the Whites, with a mother of German-Balt nobility who used to bring her boy for vacation to the remainders of the family's country estates in Latvia that stemmed from Imperial Russian times, and married to a Swedish baroness, he must lean over backwards to impress his socialist following. He was assisted by Carl Lidbom, who for a long time served as minister without portfolio and exercised considerable influence in the cabinet. Under the new leadership, Sweden entered into an era of virulently anti-American policy—paradoxically, largely an American import—that dominated the subsequent period and reached such peaks that the American ambassador at times was withdrawn. Part of this policy was an intense support for the socialist regime that took over in Chile in 1970 under President Allende. In the increasingly polarized Chilean society that developed after the takeover, the Swedish government sympathized more with the supporters of the regime seeking to destroy the managerial and middle class and to establish a dictatorship of the revolutionary Left than with the opponents of the same regime. So too did the Cuban regime that concentrated on Chile after 1970 and moved its headquarters for revolutionary activity from the Paris Cuban Embassy to the new Cuban Embassy in Santiago.[8] After the Pinochet coup of September 11, 1973, a Swedish propaganda offensive was mounted against the new regime that involved among others the Swedish International Development Aid organization.[9] Pressured by the leftist forces on which the position of the new Swedish leadership depended, the government allowed the wholesale importation to Sweden of Chilean refugees and other Latin American revolutionaries stranded by the Pinochet coup and provided language training, jobs, homes, and funds for them. By early 1974, Sweden, with a population of 8 million, had received some 400 Chilean refugees, while countries like the almost three times bigger DDR in the socialist camp and revolution-exporting Cuba had limited their intake to 70 and 100, respectively, for fear that the exiles could be a source of domestic unrest.[10] Certainly the very extremist character of many of these refugees tended to make them disrupt things in any country that offered them a place to go. The license to practice foreign politics inherent in the Papandreou line came to confer upon Sweden the character of something of a base area for staging a countercoup in Chile. The increasingly hostile Swedish attitude towards Chile was accompanied by an increasingly friendly attitude towards Cuba. After the official Kalckenberg visit to Cuba in 1971, annual aid was at a level of 2.5 million Sw Cr; by 1975, that aid had risen to 60 million Sw Cr annually in spite of the surprising Cuban re-exportation of aid to mostly African and some Asian countries.[11]

The Personnel Control Ordinance, 1969

Sweden was spared the visitation of the Second World War. The coming of that war brought an attitude of vigilance, however. In the late 1930s, the Swedish agency of interior security started to register communists and nazis. In a move to please the victorious Soviet neighbor, the registration of communists ceased in 1945, but was reinstated in 1948 in the wake of the successful operations of the activist committees in Prague. On June 19, 1963, disaster struck the inner security organization of Sweden in the form of the prosecution of Colonel Wennerström. This spy scandal, the greatest ever to affect Sweden, exposed numerous and serious shortcomings in the security system. A parliamentary committee was set up to study the guidelines for processing security questions. One result was the adoption of the Police Register Act of April 9, 1965, which contained guidelines for all such registers, even those of the inner security people. Another was the publication in 1967 of a broad report on how to strengthen inner security.[12]

The Soviet decision, after the Six-Day War, of all-out support for the Arabs, however, brought confusion.[13] Combining with the anti-American policy that was the hallmark of the new socialist leadership in Sweden, there followed a polarization with increasing leftist and increasingly leftist forces on the one side and the United States and Israel and their increasingly demoralized sympathizers on the other side. The leftists, on which the new leadership depended, made a show of force and the suggestions of the parliamentary committee were inexplicably set aside.

The Personnel Control Ordinance that was issued on June 13, 1969, to supplement the Police Register Act contained, contrary to what the committee had proposed, strict guidelines for what could be entered into the police registers, and a dramatic innovation was inserted in Article 2 by the following:

No annotation in such a register may be made on the mere basis that somebody has expressed a political opinion by belonging to an organization or in some other way.

This ordinance was followed by guidelines adopted by the National Police Board on December 17, 1970, which read in part:

It is however a well-known fact that certain political extremist movements represent views that purport to subvert democratic society by violent means. The risk is evident that a member of or sympathizer with such an organization is prepared to take part in antisocial activity. Evidently it may happen that a person is member of, or sympathizer with, such an organization without being prepared to take part in antisocial activity. If this is clear he shall not be registered.[14]

The setback for the idea of strengthening inner security was considerable, in particular in the field of fellow travelers, a category that Münzenberg had employed so masterfully in the service of Soviet policy during the Spanish civil war. All existing registration of membership in the Communist party was destroyed by the police unless the entry could be supported by supplementary information.[15] Even the military security service destroyed what duplicates it might have had.[16] The justitie ombudsman, who is not necessarily a very realistic dignitary, went as far as to criticize as "offensive" the fact that military security people attended and took notes at a major servicemen's meeting where the conscripts aired their political hostility to the armed forces. The ombudsman based his criticism, it would seem, exclusively on the fact that the politicking servicemen had voiced indignation over being supervised, but he also added, naively, that the supervision "must have appeared ridiculous to citizens of sound judgment"[17]—a view that left completely out of sight the rapidly deteriorating Swedish military situation and the consequential general demoralization of the armed forces. Military preparedness, however, was no responsibility of the ombudsman.

In May 1973, a new blow was dealt to Swedish security. At the cabinet level, as part of a more general movement shifting responsibilities from the civil and military service to the labor union bureaucracy, the decision had been taken to set up outside of the civil and military service a separate intelligence outfit called IB (for "informations Byran"), and this outfit had succeeded in disguising itself so well that even among high military men in intelligence work, its existence was not known. However, it had some contacts with Israeli intelligence. The leftist machine, associated with Palestinian militants through a group called "Action Group Palestinian Front" and headed by Mrs. Marina Stagh, set out to destroy it. On May 3, 1973, an issue of a paper of the extreme left called *Folket i Bild/Kulturfront* was published with a ten-page report on the Swedish intelligence service. This report was authored by the husband of Mrs. Stagh, Jan Guillou, a French citizen. After great confusion in government circles, Guillou and his helpers were finally arrested on October 10, 1973, on the charge of espionage. Eventually, a ten-month jail sentence was affirmed (*certiorari* denied September 1974). The matter came before the ombudsman who this time said, among other things, relating to the fact that an IB agent had joined a militant leftist organization for reconnaissance purposes: "An infiltration—because after all that is what is here at issue—into political and other associations that are not illegal, always appears as a violation of the freedom of association that is guaranteed to Swedish citizens."[18]

The Yugoslavs

Internal security, however, was also threatened by imported quarrels. The great immigration from Yugoslavia that had taken place during the 1960s brought Croat separatism with it. The political activity of the Croat separatists in Sweden, long overlooked by the Swedish police but perfectly permissible under the new Papandreou line, was sufficiently uncontrolled to make the communist government in Yugoslavia nervous. Sending in political agents to counteract the

Croat activity, it exposed itself to murder and trial in Sweden. Most attention was attracted by the Asanov trial in 1970. Yugoslav security agents reportedly succeeded in making their Croat adversaries occupy, in February 1971, the Yugoslav consulate in Gothenburg with a view to extorting the release of Miljenko Hrkac who had been sentenced to death in Yugoslavia as a Croat terrorist but who, in reality, it appears, was a Yugoslav security agent.[19] Eventually, the Croats assassinated the Yugoslav ambassador to Sweden, a former general believed to have a bloodstained past in Yugoslav security service.

This problem also went into the lap of the Swedish security service. Said the ombudsman, in a review of the task of supervising extremist organizations among certain immigrant groups:

The operations of these organizations is often not directly aimed against our country and its institutions, but against other members of the immigrant group or against the institutions of other countries in this realm. What has happened, and it is not necessary to review them, has shown that it is necessary to supervise such organizations. By itself, this should be a task for the general police. . . . Several circumstances, among others, the secret nature of these extremist organizations and their conspiratorial methods of operation make it, however, difficult for the open police to find out about their activities. Nor should it be overlooked, that some of these foreign extremist organizations have connections with certain domestic extremist movements. The security service with its special working methods is, in this respect, a better instrument, although, it too, seems to have considerable difficulties. . . . A special problem is whether or not members of foreign extremist movements should be registered at the security department.[20]

The Hijacking Incident

On September 15, 1972, an SAS airliner was hijacked by a Croat patrol and the Swedish government gave in to the demands that they release from prison seven Croat prisoners serving sentences for a number of political crimes, the most famous one being the murder of Ambassador Rolovic already referred to.

That event made the Swedish government set up, on September 22, 1972, a commission under the chairmanship of Minister Lidbom to draft a statutory law aimed at preventing, in Sweden, acts of political violence having an international background.

Revision of the Personnel Control Ordinance

The immediate result of the hijacking event was the revision of the 1969 Personnel Control Ordinance. On September 22, 1972, the famous innovation of 1969 about the nonregistration of "political opinion" was supplemented with the addition: "More precise regulations relative to the application of this rule will be issued by the King in Council." The addition thus conferred upon the government the authority to issue further directives as to the practical application of the rules for registration.

The government used the occasion to state, in a royal letter to the National Police Board, that there were organizations and groups that pursue political activity entailing the view that violence, threats, or constraint may be used as measures to achieve political goals. Certain organizations, the letter continues, have adopted programs stating that the organization shall be active in changing society by violent means. A great number of the members of such organizations may, however, be believed never to contribute to the implementation of the program by violent means. By this is meant—explains the letter—mere membership in Swedish political organizations that openly manifest a revolutionary goal shall not be grounds for registration. So far, the royal letter had merely restated the situation as it was, both in general and in relation to fellow travelers.

It was then added that, for organizations that may engage in political subversive activity that includes the use of violence, threats, or constraint, in Sweden or abroad, information concerning members or sympathizers should be entered in the police register of the security department.[21] In an interview the same day, Minister of Justice Geijer confirmed that "current membership of sympathies" should be registered.

The leftist machine, which at that time already controlled all newspapers of national distribution except one,[22] immediately reacted by noting the potential of censure in relation to aggressions overseas by "liberation" movements. In the said "conservative" daily, *Svenska Dagbladet*—which is about as "conservative" as Anthony Lewis, its permanent and almost exclusive commentator on American politics—the interview with Geijer was accompanied by the observation that the new directive meant a threat to sympathizers with foreign liberation movements.[23]

The Lidbom Report

The Lidbom Commission delivered its report on December 8, 1972.[24] In broad lines, the report proposed the enactment of a law that tried to develop, in harmony with the 1971 Montreal Convention (although the convention was not mentioned and was not at that time ratified by Sweden nor in force[25]), cooperation between the different national police forces, so that the Swedish police could act upon information received from foreign police forces. The overriding principle throughout the proposed law was that it should not deal with penal law issues, but only with the administration of aliens, thereby—as a windfall—avoiding any collision with the European Convention on Human Rights.[26] A foreigner who was suspect due to foreign police tips could be expelled from Sweden or his entry into Sweden could be refused.

Essentially, the proposed legislation attempted to make clear the conditions for taking measures against a foreigner who belonged to, or was active for, an organization or a group that one could fear would resort to violence in Sweden for political purposes. It should be possible to return such a foreigner upon arrival or to expel him from the country. It was proposed that the National Police Board should be empowered to make a list of foreigners to be expelled or returned pursuant to this rule—hereinafter referred to as the "terrorist list"—but directives on how to draw the list were to be issued by the king in council. One condition for the working of the scheme was that the foreigner could not be a political refugee. If he could not be expelled from Sweden because of political refugee status, it should be possible to issue special directives for him with limitations or conditions for his future presence in Sweden; in short, to deprive him of the license to practice politics in Sweden that followed from the Papandreou line. Furthermore, it should be possible to use measures of constraint against him. The application of the law was to be safeguarded by rules allowing Parliament special insight into its operation and control over it. The law was to be in effect for one year only, with the faculty of renewal.

The Discussion

The Lidbom Report caused an uproar in leftist quarters. This group saw their privileges obtained during the period of Palme government being eroded and they mounted a counteroffensive. The proposed drafting of a terrorist list and the basis for making entries therein was the major bone of contention. Evidently, the terrorist list was another form of a police register that seemed to follow other principles than those developed in the recent past for police registers. More specifically, the 1969 addition on "opinion registration" was missing. In popular belief, fostered by the leftist press, there existed a legal prohibition against the so-called opinion registration although, in fact, this was not quite true. The ombudsman later stated "that the rules that exist in this respect—those put in the Personnel Control Ordinance—in form only apply to the registers of the security police."[27] The language of the bill was that antiterrorist measures could be taken against a foreigner, and he could be entered into the terrorist list, if there was "a well-founded reason to believe that he belongs to or is active for a political organization or group that one may fear will in this realm resort to violent means, threats, or constraint."

In the parliamentary debate on December 11, 1972, the discussion concerned the "opinion registration" of members of Swedish organizations. Lidbom suggested for entry into the police register, members of such organizations as the Communist Confederation of Marxists-Leninists, Clarté, the Federation of Anarchists in Sweden, the Neo-Swedish movement, the Nordic Realm-party, or any other extremist group—left or right wing—that espouses resorting to violence in its program. When the bill was tabled, Lidbom defended the terrorist list idea further. Firstly, the legislation aimed only at those groups that by having already systematically used violence in past actions have proven that they will likely resort to violence in the future. Secondly, he argued that most of the persons registered will never have been in Sweden and that the information on them will be received from foreign sources such as Interpol (of which Yugoslavia is a member, incidentally) or various national police agencies. He also gave assurances that the information would be checked thoroughly. However, he admitted that the possibility still existed that foreigners could be refused entry even though they were never associated in any way with a terrorist organization. The minister pointed out that the alternative was to do nothing at all.[28]

Elwin, a Marxist penologist with seemingly free access to the pages of the big daily *Dagens Nyheter,* pointed out that what was, at first, officially aimed at activities of criminal rightist organizations was later conveniently used by security police to control members of leftist organizations and liberation movements.[29] More specifically, however, Elwin challenged the notion that "revolutionary program" and "violent means" could be equated. Every Marxist could tell—according to Elwin—that such an equation should not take place, and he suggested that Lidbom attempt to learn something from his colleague, Minister of Justice Geijer, who was believed to be, said Elwin, "one of the cabinet's two schooled Marxists."[30]

The vague language of the bill came under attack. C.G. Lidberg criticized formulas such as "a well-founded reason to believe" and "a group that one may fear." He felt that if the legislation only aimed at the groups described by Lidbom, it would not be difficult to formalize the statutory language accordingly.[31] Judge Gehlin showed his talent for absorbing guilt when he compared the use of such expressions as "well-founded reason to believe," "important for finding out," or "threatening public order and security" in the new legislation to the excuses used by totalitarian regimes to silence the politically troublesome.[32]

The fellow traveler problem was brought up. According to Lidberg, the proposed formula on membership or collective association might well affect people who, though they may belong to such organization, would never think of engaging in violent activities themselves. He went on to point out that age or physical condition may even preclude active participation for some of them.[33] Judge Gehlin picked the same point. It deviated from the principles of the Code of Procedure. Pursuant to 23:3 of the code "the prosecutor shall take over . . . as soon as somebody reasonably can be suspected of the offense." But, said Judge Gehlin, a person may be put on the terrorist list and measures of constraint of the type regulated by the code may be used against him, according to the proposed legislation, without his being associated with any specific offense. He emphasized that one would not even have to suspect that the individual was ready to use violent means, threats, or constraint.[34] So lawyers Lidberg and Gehlin wanted a return to the individualizing approach of the Code of Procedure.

So did the chief state prosecutor in his official comments on the bill. He felt that the examples given in the report regarding when measures of constraint for reconnaissance purposes were permissible were so extreme that they came very close to what was required in the code for opening a real police inquiry.

This calls for an observation. The report typified a kind of draftsmanship that had become commonplace during the socialist era of government: to trick the lay members of Parliament—incidentally now 96 percent of the membership—into adopting the bill.[35] But this time the technique back-fired.

Lidberg doubted that the reservations and clarifications mentioned in the *travaux préparatoires* (draft) were a sufficient guarantee as long as such declarations were not also reflected in the language of the statute.[36] Elwin pointed out that such a legislation allowed considerable leeway for those who applied it. He felt that, in practice, one was empowering the police to register political opinion and, in doing so, to decide who would fall into the category of "presumed terrorist."[37] The conclusion of the chief state prosecutor went the other way. It was that the examples, accepted at face value, merely showed that one could well adhere to the requirements spelled out in the Code of Procedure.

Eventually, the authors of the bill tried to fend off the opposition by stating that the legislation only required neutrality since it was directed only against foreigners who used violence on Swedish soil.[38] Lidbom eventually promised that the legislation would not be used without prior cabinet permission, except against two specified movements: "Ustasja" and "Black September." A terrorist movement acting on foreign soil to change political conditions anywhere other than Sweden remained privileged.

The act was passed on April 13, 1973. It was renewed on April 26, 1974 (SFS 1974 No. 178) and June 5, 1975 (SFS 1975 No. 355). It expired December 30, 1975, and was replaced by a slightly different structure partly integrated into the Aliens Act and partly reenacted as a separate act (see SFS 1975 Nos. 1358 and 1360, respectively).

The Application of the Act

The Terrorist List

The terrorist list was drawn up by the National Police Board pursuant to directives issued by the king in council on April 13, 1973. The following language was used in naming two *organizations*: "those organizations or groups that may be referred to as the so-called Ustasja movement" (an all-inclusive description that seems to cover everything from the purely cultural organization HOP to more militant groups such as HNO-Drina and down to HRB, the Croatian revolutionary fraternity, an outright fighting corps with military manuals and the like) and "that or those groups within the Palestinian liberation movement that may be assumed to be attached to Black September" (also a very broad description that certainly threatened parts of the pro-Palestinian movement cleverly built up in leftist circles after the Six-Day War). On September 28, 1973, new directives added to the list: "organization or group that may be referred to as the Japanese Red Army" (also an all-inclusive formula that may have meant, although this seems by no means clear, the Red Army faction or Rengo Sekigunha, in contradistinction to the Chukakuha, a middle-core faction, and the Kahumaruha, a revolutionary Marxist faction). Why the Japanese Red Army was singled out for entry at that time remains somewhat obscure. Early assertions of a Cuban-based international terrorist conspiracy[39] had been dramatically corroborated by the Lydda (Lod) Massacre of May 30, 1972, performed by a Red Army patrol for the benefit of the PFLP. Indeed, it turned out that the Red Army had already contacted the PFLP in 1968 to forge ideological links. However, a PFLP spokesman denied that Beirut was the home base of the Red Army by stating that they had not been there since 1972.[40] The following winter the Red Army faction staged several joint operations with the Arabs, the most notable of which was the one where two Japanese and a Palestinian allegedly blew up an oil refinery in Singapore.[41]

After the attack on the Stockholm Embassy of the Federal Republic of Germany in late April 1975, in which Lt. Col. Baron von Mirbach was shot, the Baader-Meinhof group was added to the list. The following formula was used: "organization or group that can be referred to as the Red Army faction, also called the Baader-Meinhof group." By this, it was presumably meant the organization known as the Red Army faction in the Federal Republic of Germany.

Thus, the list was limited to four organizations. The principle for selection of organizations has been discussed. Melander suggests that it:

... appears that a condition for being considered as a dangerous organization, according to the Antiterrorist Act, is that, on the basis of its prior activity, the organization has performed an act of political violence outside the country against which it is active. It then does not matter whether the terrorist act took place in Sweden or abroad.[42]

However, it seems that the presence of some member of, or collaborator with, the organization in Sweden is what makes it eligible for entry into the list. Tomislav Rebrina, who commanded the patrol that hijacked SAS flight 130, belonged to HNO-Drina, which thus was associated with a violent operation in Sweden. No such operation could be ascribed to Black September or the Japanese Red Army, but at the time of their insertion, group members were believed to be in Sweden.

However, one will find the list of organizations highly selective and not a very significant contribution to the international fight against terrorism. All liberation movements can be accused of resorting to politically inspired violence outside the country they have picked for an adversary, simply because it is part of the tactic to operate from a neighboring country, where discipline is maintained and contributions collected and supporters recruited under pressure that certainly involves threat of violence or outright constraint. Even if Sweden has not taken note of such disciplinary murders as those in which the Algerian FLN engaged and that surfaced in the famous Ktir Case,[43] recruitment for the Palestinian cause and the extortion of contributions under threats of violence occasionally do come to light in the Swedish university context and sometimes even are brought to the attention of the police.

It may be suggested that the list of organizations has, in reality, only a limited function. Nobody can be entered into the list as a presumed terrorist without his attachment to one of the listed organizations first being established. By the end of 1975, the list included slightly less than 80 *persons,* all of whom had whereabouts abroad. This list was, in all its versions, approved by the National Police Board *in pleno,* and copies thereof were successively submitted to the king in council.[44]

In subsequent comment, it has been asserted that the question of membership in terrorist organizations seldom acquires independent importance. This was ascribed to the fact that "it is a characteristic feature of the organizations and groups in question that they are of an extremely secret nature. . . . Experience has shown that here it is primarily other circumstances concerning the relationship of the specific person to the organization and its activity that become decisive."[45] By this is meant, presumably, that information coming from foreign police is always directed at a certain individual and includes evidence of his past activities in connection with acts for which a certain listed organization has taken credit, so that the membership cannot be said to have independent importance.

Other Issues

Returning of a presumed terrorist (Sections 1, 2, 5) has taken place only once. In late 1974, the National Police Board was informed that a presumed Croat terrorist was going to attempt to enter Sweden; the information even included when the attempt would be made. The terrorist was returned, but the case, evidently, is exceptional.[46]

Expulsion of presumed terrorists (Section 3) has been at issue in twelve cases. Board requests for expulsion have been submitted to the King in Council and have been granted in about half the cases. In 1974, decisions to expel were taken in relation to three Yugoslavs and one Japanese (Akira Kitagawa). In 1975, the decision was taken to expel another Yugoslav as well as the five-member patrol of Germans that took the West German Embassy in order to extort the release of the Baader-Meinhof defendants. In six of these cases, the requests were either turned down or withdrawn. The latter action was presumably because the alleged terrorist had left the country anyway.

In none of the Yugoslav cases could the decision to expel be executed, due to *political refugee status*. Instead, the presumed terrorists were subjected to directives with *limitations and conditions for their continued presence* in Sweden (Section 9). These directives merely established limitations relating to residence and employment, which could not be changed without prior permission. The presumed terrorist was also to register regularly with the police.[47]

According to Section 8, when the execution of a decision to expel is stayed (e.g., due to political refugee status), the question of execution may later be reconsidered. In the case of Kitagawa, the execution of the decision to expel to Japan was stayed in view of political refugee status. However, for many reasons (language and distance not the least) the decision to stay execution did not have a very solid foundation. It was considered advisable to look into the matter of "political persecution" in Japan more closely. Eventually, after some on-the-spot research, it was concluded that people could be expelled to Japan without risking political persecution. Consequently, when the Shimada case was decided (see below) in favor of expulsion, the Kitagawa decision was reconsidered and the expulsion executed.

The Shimada Case

Kyoichi Shimada was a Japanese student residing in Sweden with his wife. Occasionally, he was routinely interrogated by the police. The Japanese Embassy in Stockholm asserted that he was guilty of passport irregularities and asked the Swedish police to deprive him of the fake passport. In early February 1975, Haruyuki Mabuchi, counselor at the Japanese Embassy in Stockholm, sent a circular letter to airlines, shipping lines, and others warning them about the presence in Sweden of Shimada and identifying him as a member of the Red Army faction.[48] In late March, the Swedish Embassy in Athens received a letter signed by the Red Army threatening an attempt to release two Japanese—Nishikawa and Tohira—recently sent home from Sweden (without resort to the Antiterrorist Act). On June 27, 1975, the Carlos affair started by the murder of two French DST agents in Paris, revealing, as it developed, the worldwide terrorist connections between the Japanese, the Latin American, the Palestinian, and the Baader-Meinhof people.[49] It followed the Japanese Red Army's attack on the Swedish Embassy in Kuala Lumpur and the taking hostage of the Swedish chargé d'affaires, Bergenstrahle.[50]

This gradual buildup of events seems to have made the Shimada situation mature. The National Police Board requested his expulsion, and the decision to expel was taken on September 2, 1975. The decision was executed. Back in

Japan, however, it turned out that the case of the Japanese police against Shimada was weak, and he was detained in prison merely on charges of having obtained a false passport. At the same time, Kitagawa was expelled and flown to Japan. Since there apparently was no case against him, he was reportedly released.

The "Refugee Council"—a private group created in 1971 and chaired by a renowned leftist, Advocate Franck—set up a working group against the Antiterrorist Act with the support of similar outfits such as the Chile committee and the Africa group. This working group invited the opinion of the representative of "The International Federation for Human Rights" that reportedly has NGO status and possibly advisory functions with the United Nations. This representative, Jean Claude Luthi, said that the two Japanese had not had the opportunity to defend themselves in court.

Criticism

First of all, it has been questioned whether the Swedish Antiterrorist Act is compatible with the European Convention on Human Rights. It seems that, generally, Swedish commentators are satisfied that it is, being exclusively a regulation of aliens' rights to be in Sweden.[51] The doubts that have been voiced have concentrated on the measures of constraint, because they seem to be invoked merely on the basis of the terrorist list, and this in turn is said to be made up on the basis of political opinion, a discrimination incompatible with Article 14 of the convention.[52]

Inasmuch as there is a tendency to narrow the gap between regulating aliens' rights to be in Sweden and the rules for police inquiry, it may be pertinent to point to one difficulty with the call for international police cooperation in Article 12 of the Montreal Convention. The meaning of the term *offense* in an international criminal law context is seldom fully clear. If police forces are to cooperate, one cannot reasonably insist on interpreting "offense" in formulas such as "suspected of the offense" in 23:3 as referring only to a violation of the local police force's domestic criminal law that takes place within the domestic territory, because that will simply defeat the cooperation. "Offense" must be interpreted in an international spirit.

The Swedish legislature has shied away from the fellow traveler problem and has been lucky inasmuch as nothing has happened that has focused attention on it. It must be recalled, however, that these are guerrilla operations that always tactically rely a great deal on passive supporters and sympathizers. How much is contributed to the success of a terrorist operation by (1) a farmer in whose barn the explosives are found; (2) a fourteen-year-old girl on whose person is found a letter directing her to purchase medicine for the terrorists, together with a sum of money; or (3) a man who has on his person a ledger that clearly is a tax collection book for a political sector of the terrorist organization? None of these people is himself prepared to blow people up or otherwise resort to violence; still their services are essential to the terrorist operation. A fellow traveler's services are valuable, as a maildrop, a haven, a courrier, or a warner. Sometimes they may have the important function unknowingly; for example, the British girls who smuggled bombs on board aircraft that had been planted in their luggage by terrorist friends without their knowledge. There may be special reasons why Sweden has restricted the application of the Antiterrorist Act, but the country is left unprepared for terrorism that consists of more than isolated instances and resembles war on foreign battlefields.

The basic weakness in the Swedish approach has turned out to be the condition of political refugee status because that has prevented the execution of a decision to expel. The comment of the chief prosecutor in Stockholm seems pertinent:

Since it justifiably can be said that, in most cases under the new Act, those foreigners to which it applies are such as may invoke political activity at the one and same time as grounds for returning and expulsion, on the one side, and on a bar for such measures on the other.[53]

Political refugee status should be granted to the presumed terrorist, if he risked "political persecution" in the country to which he was to be sent. What was meant by this extremely imprecise formula was very unclear; still it was pivotal in the matter. The heavily leftist Swedish mass media were almost able to freeze the application of the act to the Baader-Meinhof group by singling out the Federal Republic of Germany in an attack that focused on the social monopoly on violence and on attorneys' privileges in communicating with clients, as a country that had lost the rule of law.[54] If that was synonymous with "political persecution," the murderous squad could look forward to some time in a Swedish jail (probably no longer than masterspy Col. Wennerström, who eventually was pardoned by the Palme government) and thereafter remain in Sweden on social welfare, if not otherwise. So what was meant by "political persecution"?

The campaign against South Africa and the success of a more general human rights movement, on this point, had married into a most surprising formula. Melander has maintained that it would be political persecution if somebody risked search of premises, search of person, wire tapping, and so forth on the basis of his political opinion. "It is difficult to understand," says Melander, "why a violation of human rights cannot be considered to be persecution, of course on condition that this violation is founded on . . . political opinion. To take the Swiss example relating to the former prohibition for women to take part in general elections, this certainly was a violation of the declaration of human rights, but it could not be considered persecution, since the prohibition was not based on race, nationality, etc., but on sex, which is not mentioned by the Refugee Convention as a basis for persecution. And it seems right to consider there is persecution in the case of a colored citizen of Rhodesia, who is excluded from the right to participate in general elections due to his race."[55]

Such definitions of "political persecution" make it hard to send a presumed terrorist anywhere. Moynihan, the U.S. delegate to the United Nations, has reminded us that there are no more than two dozen genuine democracies remaining in the world. The rest are nations that have adopted or accepted autocratic forms of government, socialist or not. He was prepared to produce a list of forty-five military governments and thirty-five other governments installed by military coups. Certainly, all of these would fail to meet the test suggested by Melander. On the other hand, the rule of law might conceivably be a lot better in some of these countries than in the genuine democracies, because the rule of the majority is no guarantee that the majority will stick to the laws it has created. Furthermore, a foreigner may well travel in a country without participating in its general elections and without having any reason to complain of any "political persecution" because he abstains from politics. When the Swedish government reached the decision to send Shimada and Kitagawa back to Japan, it appears to have been a move in a sounder policy direction; it does not seem to have been sound policy to make Sweden the haven for all revolutionaries in the world.

12 Political Prisoners and Terrorists in American Correctional Institutions

Edith Flynn

In the last decade, Americans have become increasingly aware of political crime and political criminals. The specter of the Chicago Seven trial, the painful Watergate affair, and the bizarre destruction surrounding the activities of the Symbionese Liberation Army have heightened the public's sensitivity to the entire issue of political crimes. Interestingly, the concept of political crime is an old and recurring one in the history of mankind. Yet, the topic of political crime has been largely overlooked by criminologists. Their inattention to the problem is not easy to explain. Granted, street crimes, violence, and property offenses far outweigh political crime in terms of frequency and amount of damage that is done. Even though political prisoners capture the headlines, the number of their depredations is small when compared with the sum of crimes recorded in the public annals.

Nevertheless, there are sufficient reasons to focus our attention on political crime in general and on acts of terrorism in particular. The use of terrorism as an instrument of political protest and political action is an invasion of the state's monopoly on the use of force. No political authority can long hope to survive prolonged, broad-scale, and successful terrorism without either giving way to conditions of anarchy or resorting to repressive measures characteristic of totalitarian regimes. The prospect of spreading terror and violence is sufficient reason for criminologists to study these phenomena. Only when they do so, can they hope to gain a better knowledge of the forces that generate political violence, and the characteristics of persons who engage in it, and to begin the process of identifying measures for the prevention of terrorism. Minimally, we should be able to limit the physical and social harm inflicted on the population and assure the survival of our social institutions.

The purpose of this brief exposition is to focus on the use of institutionalization as a means of coping with political prisoners and terrorists. We will therefore refrain from discussing the many complex and larger issues of political crime and terrorism and limit ourselves to the following issues: (1) the prevalence of political prisoners in the American correctional system; (2) an analysis of the special problems related to the political prisoner's presence in the criminal justice system; and (3) some possible solutions to the problems of institutional management of political prisoners and political terrorists. Finally, the problem of the political prisoner in the United States appears to be sufficiently different from the problems of political prisoners and terrorists in other countries, such as

87

Chile, Brazil, Greece, Indonesia, Czechoslovakia, and Third World countries, to warrant a separate discussion.

The Issue of Prevalence

There is no statistical information available as to the number of political prisoners that may be present on any one day in the vast American correctional apparatus that includes federal, state, and local systems. The reason is that the term *political crime* has no meaning as such in American criminal law (with the exception of the special provisions governing the extradition of political prisoners).[1] There are, of course, a variety of crimes against the state, such as treason, espionage, rebellion, and sedition, that have political implications. None of these activities, however, are major problems in American society. The political crimes at issue here invariably involve the international violation of penal law. As such, the political criminal can be differentiated from the common criminal in that the former is presumed to be motivated by altruistic goals and believes that his or her violation of the penal law is justifiable or even required by some higher purpose. The common criminal, in contrast, is supposedly motivated by the pursuit of private and selfish goals. As a result of this differentiation, we can now distinguish between three types of criminal activity: (1) common crime, which is a violation of penal law for private gain or personal satisfaction (e.g., armed robbery, rape, and so forth); (2) pure political crime, which is the violation of political penal law (e.g., treason, espionage, and so forth); and (3) mixed political crime, which is the commission of a common crime in pusuit of political purpose (e.g., the bombing of a government building as an expression of political protest).

Even though exact information as to the prevalence of political prisoners in the American correctional system is not available, it is estimated that their number is very small. Nonetheless, correctional administrators and scholars have come to recognize that their presence has had an impact on prison life and has contributed to the politicization of the American prison and jail. Since the racial conflicts endemic in American society continue unabated in the prison setting, the issue of politicization has become even more blurred. To be sure, recent instances of prison violence have taken on new nuances. See for example, the accounts of the riots at Attica, Lucasville, and Holmesburg (Pennsylvania), to name some of the recent major conflagrations. Any quick perusal of these accounts will reveal that, as a concomitant to the political quality of prison conflict, the escalation of recent confrontations at these prisons has put the nature of violence into a context far different and exceedingly more dangerous than the simple predatory attacks on fellow prisoners and staff that used to characterize most prison violence in the past. It is relatively easy to control the predatory activities of a small number of inmates who prey on, exploit, and intimidate fellow inmates, but it is quite another matter to deal with violence directed at staff and the institution itself, by a small group, whose existence or specific membership may be unknown until a violent outburst occurs. The situation becomes exacerbated when such a group can represent their cause as one that is carried out on behalf of all inmates and one that can claim the moral support of like-minded groups on the outside. There is considerable evidence to suggest that correctional management has not been particularly adept at controlling heretofore comparatively stable prison conditions. It is therefore easy to assume that prison management will be even less adequate for the control of guerrilla or urban warfare operations aimed at the disruption of prisons or at the destruction of the entire criminal justice system, should such developments come about at some future point.

Specific Problems related to the Presence of Political Prisoners in the Criminal Justice System

At the present time, there is considerable speculation among correctional administrators (but little concrete proof) that there may be a direct transfer of violence from the community into the prison and from the prison back into the community by groups who advocate violent solutions to social problems.[2] Given a considerable degree of social unrest and the fact that prisons and jails constitute microcosms (albeit unnatural ones) of society at large, such assumptions appear to have face validity. First, there is some evidence that at least part of the Symbionese Liberation Army had its origins in the prisons of California: Soledad, Folsom, San Quentin, and most importantly, at the California Medical Facility in Vacaville. It was at Vacaville that the Black Cultural Association was formed in 1968, whence the SLA emerged from an unholy union of convicts and their young, white, middle-class visitors and admirers. Second, well-organized ethnic groups have been recently identified as a major, serious source of prison violence in California.[3] A growing number of assaults on staff are believed to be undergirded by a revolutionary ethic. Also, the way violence is expressed in correctional institutions appears to have undergone a change; collective violence has been replaced, to some degree, by the hit-and-run tactics of guerrilla warfare. Nonetheless, ideologically motivated violence must be considered as a minor source of institutional discord when compared to other known causes. Violence and disorder resulting from organized gangs, individual emotional disturbance, and the peculiar nature of the prison subculture combine to far outweigh any violence attributable to revolutionary or terrorist-inspired ideology. For example, there is no evidence to support administrative contentions that the Attica tragedy was a consequence of a radical, political conspiracy. The same observation applies to any of the other prison riots of the recent past.

In the light of this discussion, the problem of the political prisoner in the correctional system in America is real but at this point of manageable proportions. It is unlikely, therefore, that the American prison and jail system should be regarded as seriously threatened by imminent political upheaval. Nor should we expect the impending disintegration of the criminal justice system under the onslaught of radicals or revolutionary liberators. Nevertheless, it is important to recognize that correctional institutions can make rather useful targets for revolutionaries and may therefore become vulnerable unless appropriate steps are taken to ward off such developments.

Institutional Management of Political Prisoners

A discussion of institutional management of political prisoners and particularly of solutions to the problem of violence such prisoners might cause can be little more than an overview of recommendations that are well known and familiar to administrators and scholars alike. Most importantly, the measures are applicable to any prison and jail setting and regardless of their underlying motives, are designed to reduce conflict and violence.

Remedies for the Basic Causes of Dissent

It is painful but necessary to examine the phenomenon of the political prisoner and terrorist in terms of the larger issues. For example, if we find a real discrepancy between the claims of social justice and the injustice inflicted by the criminal justice apparatus, then the revolutionary cause can place the system not only on a moral defensive but can also enlist the sympathetic support of large elements of the public.[4] This is especially true when it can be shown that the criminal justice system, in general, and the prison system, in particular, are instruments of racial injustice. If we find that the existing social order—supported by the criminal justice system—benefits one particular social group, while it discriminates against another social group, then it may be well advised to realign existing power and opportunity structures, particularly if we take seriously such historically celebrated values as equity, justice, and equal opportunity for all.

Creating a Sound and Humane Prison

At present, there is a desperate need to improve the quality of prison and jail life. Too many administrators are inept, too many correctional staff untrained, underpaid, undereducated, and frequently prejudiced. The potential for conspiracies under these conditions is great. Criminal and antisocial activities are rampant in institutions now. It is easy to speculate what purposeful, intelligent, and politically motivated prisoners could accomplish under existing prison and jail conditions, were they inclined to wreak havoc.

Introducing Basic Changes in the Prison and Jail Subculture

The characteristics of the prison subculture need not be elaborated here. Suffice it to say, that everything possible will need to be done to destroy that subculture. The megaprison of 1,000 to 3,000 or more inmates must go. It is a standing invitation to violence and anarchy, and it is totally destructive to the inmates and staff within. We need a much more selective application of the sanction of incarceration, not an increase of that sanction, as is presently so frequently proposed in the United States. Those who must be incarcerated for the protection of society should be accommodated in small, manageable institutions. These institutions should be broken down into self-sufficient modularized living units and should feature constructive work and education programs that have tangible value for the life outside. Correctional staff need to be reeducated and trained to overcome their traditional resistance to change, their characteristic insensitivity to the problems of minorities, and their blatant prejudice. Staff will need to become racially representative of the inmate populations. Waiting for affirmative action programs or civil service to accomplish that change simply will not do the job. The current phenomenon of minority prisoners, being herded about by armed members of the majority group, is administratively untenable and morally unsound.

Introduction of Equity and Justice into the Correctional Process

At present, the correctional system is replete with injustice. Prisoners should be entitled to due process when being dealt with for violations of institutional rules. Penalties should be humanely and reasonably administered. The inhumanity of most isolation units should give way to more productive dispositions. The problem of the indeterminate sentence and the arbitrariness of parole boards will need to be dealt with. Prisoners should receive prevailing wages for work performed and not be forced to engage in slave labor as is presently the case.

Restraint in the Use of Security and Control Measures

Given the general construction of most correctional institutions, complete control over inmates can only be achieved when inmates' activities are reduced to a bare minimum, a condition that is recognized by most administrators as inherently unstable and ultimately generative of violence. California reports on its two-year experience with the application of various restrictive controls, including the almost complete shutdown of four of its major adult institutions: These controls were wholly counterproductive and resulted in the use of more makeshift weapons and a shift of violence from the general population to the security units.[5] From a behavioral perspective, this turn of events was predictable, but now that the evidence regarding the effects of repression and isolation is available, it should receive the widest possible dissemination so that other correctional systems can avoid such mistakes, which are so costly in economic and human terms.

In conclusion, the relatively small number of political prisoners—once identified by the system—would make their repression in the institution relatively easy, but oppressive controls can never be basic solutions. The understanding of the phenomenon of political crime, the political prisoner, and the political terrorist is not apt to come without an understanding of the remedies for the basic causes of political discontent. There are few reasons to assume, however, that the recommendations outlined above will be followed. While a blueprint to correctional reform exists in the form of the *Corrections Report* of the National Advisory Commission on Criminal Justice Standards and Goals,[6] the prevailing winds spell regression and not reform for criminal justice and corrections in America. Minimum mandatory sentences, more incarceration of offenders, not less, and a general get-tough policy seem to be the order of the day. It is unlikely, therefore, that warnings against repression will be heeded and that the corrections process will for once become humanized.

13

Terrorism and Criminal Justice Operations in the Federal Republic of Germany

Erich Corves

In the Federal Republic of Germany, it is by now a well-accepted fact that terrorism and air piracy include phenomena of very different types that also stem from quite different roots. A substantial number of these crimes—which, according to my observations, is decreasing in my country—must be considered in the same category as the classic crimes against property: armed bank robberies, planned or even spontaneous taking of hostages, kidnapping for the purpose of extorting financial payments from private persons or from the public authorities, and similar crimes. What is perhaps new in this connection is the unscrupulous application of novel means of violence and of new technical possibilities, such as the threat of raids, for purposes of extortion, on public utility installations such as railways, waterworks, and power plants (even atomic).

As long as these dangerous crimes of violence are lacking a specific political motivation we are, no doubt, in a sphere where control is the task of classic crime policy. As such, these crimes could be dealt with by using that policy's methods and possibilities. In this connection, it is quite certain that the increased technical possibilities available to criminals must be countered by the application of appropriate technical facilities in defence thereof.

However, there has been an increasing prevalence in politically motivated terrorism to the extent that such activities are well in the foreground nowadays. The question of whether, and if so, to what extent, this phenomenon can be dealt with by the traditional arsenal of our police organizations and tactics, the provisions of criminal law and the law of criminal procedure, and by the traditional forms of the law of penal execution will still have to be examined. The tactics of operations and the reactions will have to be different, depending on the political conditions in individual countries, the existing social and economic circumstances, the strength of terrorist groups, and the degree of support terrorists may possibly find among portions of the population. These considerations alone, if nothing else, will show that there can be no panacea— neither one that is internationally applicable nor one that is meant for a specific individual country. Any strategy of defense must necessarily be a flexible one if it is to counter terrorism with any prospect of success.

In the Federal Republic of Germany, there has been an attempt to improve, on all levels, the prerequisites that are considered essential for an effective suppression of terrorist activities. Let me start with that field in which I participated directly.

Substantive Criminal Law

In Germany, the provisions of substantive criminal law on murder, bodily injury, crimes with explosives, other crimes dangerous to the community, robbery, and demand with threats and extortion have generally been considered sufficient to enable the courts to severely punish terrorist acts of violence. In spite of this, a number of new definitions of offenses or more severe punishment have recently been provided for in order to fill any imaginable gaps in the protection afforded by the criminal law and possibly also to obtain a stronger general preventive effect (in the sphere of crimes that are not politically motivated). For example, the Eleventh and Twelfth Criminal Law Reform Acts, both dated December 16, 1971, should be mentioned: Provisions of the German Criminal Code, namely Sections 239a and 239b on extortionate kidnapping and taking of hostages, were newly inserted or amended, and high minimum penalties were provided for such offenses.

Still in the legislative process in 1976 were proposals in a Fourteenth Criminal Law Reform Act with rephrased criminal provisions (1) on disturbance of the public peace by threatening with crime; (2) on the advocation of, and incitement to, crimes; and (3) on faking criminal offenses, in particular by raising false alarms on bomb attacks or other attacks, which have turned out to be severe disturbances to the activities of the police. The final versions of these proposals cannot be foreseen at this stage. Similar considerations apply to another bill that is to provide an addition to the present crime of founding a criminal organization, through a new section, 129a, on the "founding of terrorist organizations" with increased penalties. Once these provisions have been enacted, it may safely be assumed that not only all acts of violence but also any behavior detrimental to society that may contribute to the development of terrorism will effectively be covered by criminal law.

Law of Criminal Procedure

In this field, many difficulties arose, particularly in connection with the big trials of terrorists. The necessary guarantees, granted to all accused persons in a state governed by the rule of law, were abused excessively, in particular by the participation of lawyers who made themselves accomplices of their clients.

In view of the differences in the systems of procedural law, I think it would be of little avail if this field were discussed in detail. Nevertheless, it should be mentioned briefly that by an act of December 20, 1974, new provisions on the exclusion of the attorney from the defense and on the continuance of the trial in cases where the accused's unfitness to stand trial was brought about through his own fault (for example by a hunger strike) were created. In dispute is how far beyond this further statutory provisions—for example, on the supervision of contacts between defense counsel and client and on the enlarged police powers of the court during the trial—are necessary. As to this point, Parliament has several different drafts before it; their final fate cannot be foreseen at present.

In connection with the law of criminal procedure, I should like to mention some rules—partly belonging to substantive law, partly to procedural law—that are designed to make it possible to ignore the otherwise strictly applicable principle of legality and to promise members of a terrorist group, who are willing to give evidence, to mitigate their punishment or to exempt them from punishment. This is important because in the Federal Republic of Germany the prosecution is under a statutory obligation to take action in respect of *all* criminal offenses.

The above-mentioned Sections 239a and 239b of the German Criminal Code already provide for the possibilities of mitigating punishment if the offender releases the victim and relinquishes the desired ransom. Similar considerations apply to the attack on aviation under Section 316c of the German Criminal Code and to some comparable crimes. It is a real concern of crime policy to create, in this respect, a psychological stimulation for the offender to give up his plan. For this reason, similar possibilities have also been provided for in the new criminal provision on terrorist organizations.

It is still disputed in our country to what extent beyond the above a rule is required that provides for a kind of crown witness similar to that under Anglo-American law. Some people expect such a provision would create a greater possibility of breaking into terrorist groups than was possible before. I myself harbor doubts in this respect. However, it should be recalled that even under current law, in several cases the offender's guilt was proved by accomplices who were willing to give evidence, and some extension of the possibilities for this to occur is certainly desirable.

 Police Action

This field, I think, is the most important for an effective suppression of terrorism. The success achieved so far in the Federal Republic of Germany is, to my mind, due to a number of essential measures:

1. A considerable increase of police personnel—in particular, the establishment of special task forces with thorough special training (psychological training and training in marksmanship, karate, and other subjects);
2. Highly improved technical equipment (both for the special task forces and for other police forces) that guarantees speedy and effective action;
3. Better coordination between the police forces of the Federal Laender and the staff of the Federal Criminal Investigation Office, who have developed specific methods and means of investigation that have essentially contributed to making the operations of recent years successful;

4. The extension of preventive measures—in particular, observation of those sources that experience has shown are the support for the violent criminals in that they are provided with apartments, garages, vehicles, money, identity papers, and the like.

In connection with the last item, one must, of course, pay attention to the difficult problem of bringing an effective protection of society into harmony with the protection of the individual rights to freedom; in the Federal Republic of Germany, people are particularly sensitive to a restriction of such rights.

It is the very field of operation tactics and technical cooperation that, I am sure, is among those in which an international exchange of experience appears to promise special success.

Evaluation of Experience

Of course, effectiveness in combatting terrorism presupposes that all the experience gained will be evaluated carefully and exchanged in order to employ all the given facilities most effectively according to the circumstances of the actual individual cases. Such evaluation and exchange occurs, first of all, within the scope of the training of the police and other organs engaged in combatting terrorism. A systematic evaluation will make it easier in the future to find the proper reaction. As early as 1972 a seminar lasting several days was held at the police academy at Hiltrup; on that occasion, numerous persons who had themselves been directly engaged in the operation could exchange their experiences regarding the police tactics in the case of kidnapping, taking of hostages, and extortions.

Of special interest, I think, is a work completed last year by Wolfgang Salewski entitled *Luftpiraterie (Verlauf, Verhalten Hintergründe)* [Air Piracy (Course of Events, Behavior, Background)].[1] Relying on thorough interviews with Lufthansa pilots, copilots, and other crew members who had been victims when hostages were taken, Salewski has attempted to study regularities in the course of events and the psychological situation of the skyjackers, as well as the possibilities for proper reactions. As a result of this study, skyjackers are considered subject to normal psychological conditions as far as stress and attrition are concerned. Salewski has concluded that there is a so-called "affect graph," or average times of psychological attrition that occur after six to twelve hours in the case of individual offenders and after roughly four to six days in the case of groups of five to six offenders. According to the study, when hostages are taken, it is during the first two hours that the risk of uncontrolled acts of violence by the kidnappers is greatest. Salewski makes the following recommendations:

During the initial stages of a skyjacking, not to undertake anything against the terrorists, but not to ingratiate oneself with them either;

In the next stages, to deepen the contacts by personal talks and talks on technical matters;

To have the contacts between the ground and the terrorists run mainly through the aircraft commander;

To disguise any tricks and tactics of delay;

To give the terrorists the feeling that they will achieve their target, at least in part;

Where specific demands are refused, to shift responsibility into *force majeure;*

In the case of groups, to bring disorder into the leadership structure;

To engage in activities from outside (e.g., assault) only when the aircraft is grounded and the terrorists are psychologically worn down;

To gain time.

We may safely assume that some of these findings can well be applied to other cases where hostages are taken in buildings or trains.

Studies of this or a similar kind should be included in an international exchange of experience. It seems to me that just such studies, which may be important for tactics and strategy of suppression, are even more important than the exchange of technical experience regarding the securing of clues, the evaluation of clues, and similar knowledge.

International Cooperation

Politically motivated acts of violence distinguish themselves to an increasing extent by the fact that the criminals who commit them can avail themselves of ever closer contacts on an international level. These contacts are particularly facilitated in Europe by the immense masses of tourists and the fact that the frontier controls have accordingly been reduced.

The reasons for these increased contacts of terrorists in foreign countries are manifold. There is, first, the access to military training in, for example, camps of Al Fatah or in other places. I should also mention the winning over of countries prepared to accept hostages or terrorists and to allow the procurement of weapons and explosives and the establishment of strongholds and contact agencies. Last but not least, I must also mention the campaigns of sympathy for politically motivated criminals that are frequently organized on an international level.

The international bond has become stronger and stronger since 1972; the majority of the crimes that have aroused international interest were of a transfrontier nature or were committed with the participation of foreign offenders. This international cooperation on the part of the terrorists and their assistants requires an equivalent cooperation in the fight against them. Such cooperation may be affected by enlarging:

1. The system of agreements and treaties (extradition treaties, obligations to punish certain crimes, *aut dedere aut punire,* definition of "political offenses," and so forth);
2. The contacts between the prosecution authorities and the exchange of scientific and technological experience and knowledge.

In regard to the first item in this list, it is hardly necessary to go into detail regarding the relevant multilateral conventions. I take for granted that everyone knows the Tokyo Convention of September 14, 1963, on Offenses and Certain Other Acts Committed on Board Aircraft, the Hague Convention of December 16, 1970, and the Montreal Convention of September 23, 1971, for the Suppression of Unlawful Acts Against the Security of Civil Aviation. We should urge as worldwide a ratification of these conventions as possible. This recommendation also applies to the U.N. Convention for the Protection of Diplomatic Agents of December 14, 1973.

In connection with this list item, I should like to go into some detail regarding the endeavors made to achieve cooperation within the Council of Europe. Here I must refer to Resolution (74) 3 of the Committee of Ministers on international terrorism, in which endeavors are made to exhaust the possibilities of extraditing such criminals and to require the application of the principle *aut dedere aut punire.* An ad hoc committee of the European Committee on Crime Problems is dealing thoroughly with these problems and has not only prepared a detailed questionnaire on each country's national legislation and court practice regarding terrorism (the replies to which are expected to make a considerable contribution to the exchange of experience) but it has also prepared the draft of a Convention of the Council of Europe that will serve to realize the aforementioned aims.[a] It is true that we should not close our eyes to the fact that any endeavors in this geographical region will mean only a limited contribution as long as certain countries, in particular in the Middle East, readily grant asylum to political assassins. Cooperation in these areas may only come about if the pressure of public opinion all over the world gradually has some effect.

In regard to the second item listed above, I have repeatedly mentioned the benefits of cooperation between prosecution authorities in the two previous

[a]This convention was published and opened for signature in January 1977—Eds.

sections. Such cooperation will have to stand the test internationally, starting within INTERPOL through the exchange of scientific and technological experience and knowledge. This exchange should include not only personal contacts between the officials and agencies directly engaged in the combat and the persons making relevant scientific and, in particular, criminological studies, but also the ready supply of material as evidence, expert opinions, and the like for the purpose of criminal prosecution in other countries.

Success and Failure in the Federal Republic of Germany

I wish to mention first some figures regarding the victims of terrorist acts in my country. So far twelve persons have been killed, a hundred have been victims of attempted murder, and eighty-seven persons have been injured in bomb attacks and shoot-outs.

Until now, 75 of the offenders and their assistants have been convicted with final and binding effect; another 49 have not yet been convicted with final and binding effect; 88 persons are in custody on remand awaiting trial; and 32 are wanted on the strength of warrants of arrest issued by judges. Investigation proceedings are pending against some 250 persons. These figures show that some substantial success has already been achieved in combatting terrorism, but they also show that there is no reason to assume that this phenomenon is already a matter of the past in our country.[b]

Possible Further Measures

An analysis of the experience gained so far shows, in my opinion, that an essential handicap for the prosecution authorities lies in the following facts: In all cases of politically motivated terrorism, the state has to face, as a rule, a fanatic minority who has started to destroy or conquer a society against which they have practically declared war—a war in which they fight with all possible means and in which they themselves are not prepared to obey any rules. In the modern industrial nations, this "war" is brought by the terrorists into a highly technical, highly specialized, and thus extremely vulnerable organism. A state that is governed by the rule of law must, however, unless it wishes to give itself up, defend itself in this war by strictly legal means.

In this connection, the idea suggests itself that such a "quasi-war" should be countered by means of power similar to those that are available to militants at war. But I think an express warning in this respect should be given, because the terrorists would achieve, thereby, the very object they are striving for, namely,

[b]In April 1977, since this chapter was written, the federal prosecutor in charge of many of these trials, Siegfried Buback, was assassinated—Eds.

to be recognized not as criminals but as "militants." I do not want to express my view as to how this problem should be viewed in those countries in which terrorism has brought about conditions bordering on civil war. I am sure that under such circumstances further considerations would have to be made.

However, as far as the conditions in my country are concerned, we must ask ourselves whether anything could really be gained by proclaiming a kind of "emergency." What means of power should be employed? For example, should the principle of relativity no longer be applicable? How and when could we find out in each case whether terrorist activities are undertaken by "ordinary" criminals or by politically motivated offenders? Who should be authorized to proclaim such an "emergency" or "quasi-war"? What legal limitation of the prerequisites would be possible and practicable at all? I think these questions clearly indicate that there are hardly any possibilities of solving this problem in this way.

However, it seems to me to be important to obtain clarity on one point regarding the powers of those who are engaged in the fight against terrorists, in particular against persons taking hostages. In a war, the leader of a task force will know exactly what statutory rules he has to obey. If, however, the leader of a task force that is supposed to free hostages orders that a well-aimed lethal shot be fired, he frequently does not know whether or not he will later have to answer a charge of manslaughter before a court.

This should not be misunderstood to mean that I consider the lethal shot to be the proper reaction in each case; what is proper can only be the result of carefully weighing the psychological situation, the risks, the possibilities of sham or real yielding, and so on. The responsible persons cannot, after all, be relieved of their responsibility for decisions that may have serious results and that will frequently have to be taken quickly. This should, however, be confined to the moral and political responsibilities. I think that the state is obliged to supply these persons who have direct responsibility with unambiguous statutory rules so that a measure ordered in the course of operations by that person, to his best knowledge and belief, cannot lead to his being brought before a criminal court. However, such a clarification must be made within the scope of the police law applicable in the respective country, unambiguously and in accordance with the requirements of a state governed by the rule of law.

To my mind, the lethal shot can only be the *ultima ratio* where tactics of protraction and delay, psychological influence for surrender, sham, or partial meeting of demands are of no avail. This is the point where technology comes into play, where it must search for and develop means that will, like a flash of lightning, put the offender out of action without endangering the hostages. What I have in mind is, for example, "chemical mace," lasers, and the like. In this respect, cooperation should take place both in the sphere of development and in the exchange of experience in order to make this possibility bear fruit everywhere as soon as possible.

In spite of the necessity for flexible reaction, it should not be left out of consideration that, on principle, a tendency not to yield to extortion demands is more suitable to prevent future acts than a decision *exclusively* meant to save human lives in an individual case. What may at first appear to be success in an individual case may have some disastrous effect in the long run. In this connection we must also bear in mind any effects reaching into the sphere of "ordinary" crime. It will not be infrequent, therefore, that the danger to potential future victims may carry more weight than quickly saving, presumably with no risk, persons in the hands of criminals at the moment.

14 The Facts on Internment in Northern Ireland

Kevin Boyle,
Tom Hadden,
and *Paddy Hillyard*

The security forces in Northern Ireland have always had the power to arrest and detain persons suspected of terrorist activity. But the legal provisions for this purpose under the old Special Powers Act were somewhat confusing, particularly in respect of members of the armed forces. In the aftermath of the initial internment operation of August 1971, the legality of many of the arrests which had been made was challenged in the high court, where it was held that those exercising the emergency powers must nonetheless fulfill the ordinary common-law requirement of informing the person arrested of the reason for his arrest.

The main concern of the Diplock Committee was to simplify the formal procedures for arrest to avoid problems of this kind, particularly where the arrest was made by young soldiers rather than legally experienced policemen. The committee recommended that members of the armed forces should have power to arrest, without warrant, any person suspected of involvement in or having information about terrorist offenses and to detain him for up to four hours for the purpose of establishing his identity (para. 49).

These recommendations were duly enacted in the Northern Ireland (Emergency Provisions) Act of 1973. In simple terms, the current position is that the army may arrest and question any suspected terrorist for a period of four hours, after which he must either be released or handed over to the police for formal charging or for a further period of questioning, up to the limit of seventy-two hours. Both in the report of the Diplock Committee (para. 50) and in the Act (Section 16), it was made clear that, once identity had been established, the detention and questioning of any person was to be directed only to the person's movements and knowledge in respect of specific terrorist incidents.

"Military Security" and "Police Prosecution"

The spirit of this limitation has not been observed in practice. The army has made use of its four-hour power of arrest to mount a massive communal screening operation in the main Catholic/Republican areas. Large numbers of innocent persons have been arrested and questioned in these areas on no other

This chapter is reprinted by permission. From Kevin Boyle, Tom Hadden, and Paddy Hillyard, "The Facts on Internment," *Fortnight*, no. 94 (Belfast: Fortnight Publications Ltd., 1974), pp. 9-12.

ground than their residence and therefore their presumed knowledge of terrorist organizations and activities there. The Royal Ulster Constabulary (RUC), on the other hand, would appear to have maintained the traditional police approach to arrest and questioning on specific charges, except insofar as it has become involved, through its Special Branch officers, in the processing of army arrests. This distinction between what may be termed the "military security" approach and the "police prosecution" approach is, in our view, crucial to an understanding of the way in which the Emergency Provisions Act has been operated. The basic difference between army and police practice amounts, in our view, to a systematic abuse by the army of the powers which the Diplock Committee and the Westminster Parliament intended to give it.

It is, we believe, the policy of the army to maintain as complete a record as is practicable of the whole population of all militant Republican areas. This covers not only the names and current places of residence of everyone in the area but also a wide range of personal and political information about those suspected of any form of active political or terrorist activity. The basic filing system is maintained at battalion headquarters, but the main details are also forwarded to the headquarters of the Northern Ireland Command at Lisburn and used as the foundation for the planning of the whole army security operation.

It is obviously important that the information in this system should be maintained in an up to date and accurate form. All army units are therefore under orders to report any observed changes in local population and its activities. Meticulous observation and recording of this kind, however, is not regarded as sufficiently accurate or productive. Army units, we believe, are expected to "screen" all potential terrorists in their area every nine months or so. This screening process is carried out through the army's power to arrest and question for up to four hours any person suspected of terrorist activity under Section 12 of the Emergency Provisions Act and to question (but not arrest) any person as to his identity and movements and as to his knowledge of terrorist incidents under Section 16 of this Act. These two separate powers, however, appear to have been conflated into an assertion of a single power to arrest and question any person for the four-hour period.

The primary subjects of this screening process are those persons who are listed on army files as "wanted" and whose descriptions and photographs are issued to all soldiers. Soldiers are also expected to take advantage of the local situation to arrest, for screening, other potential troublemakers whenever the occasion arises; for instance, if they are found outside late at night or otherwise appear to be acting suspiciously or aggressively. And if for any reason the flow of "normal" screening arrests from any particular street or district dries up to such an extent that the information on that area is deemed to be no longer adequate for "operational" purposes, a specific arrest operation may be undertaken for the purpose of bringing the files up to date. This practice may help to explain the occasional arrest operations, such as occurred, for instance, in the Creggan area in May 1974 in which suspects appear to have been selected at random, which have given rise to widespread local resentment.

Once arrested, the person concerned will be brought to the unit's screening center where he will be handed over to the military police, given a quick medical examination and then brought before the unit's intelligence specialists. He will then be questioned for anywhere from five to ten minutes to several hours, both on his own and his family's and friends' movements and on his knowledge, if any, of any recent incidents or activities in the area. If any useful leads arise in the course of questioning or if any admissions are made, the subject may then be handed over to the police for formal charging, or for further questioning under the seventy-two-hour provision referred to above. The second stage in the pretrial process under the Emergency Provisions Act begins with the handing over of a suspect to the joint army and RUC Special Branch holding and interrogation center at Castlereagh in Belfast, or similar centers elsewhere in the province. Here the suspect will again be medically examined and then produced for intermittent interrogation. This may be focussed either on the specific incident for which he may be charged, with a view to securing a sufficient admission of confession to ensure his conviction in court proceedings, or else more generally directed to supplementing the flow of information to the security forces on terrorist activities and organization. It is at this stage that the decision is made whether the suspect is to be put on trial before a Diplock court on specific criminal charges or whether an interim custody order will be made against him, with a view to putting the case before the commissioners for longer-term detention without trial. It is our understanding that the decision whether or not to prefer criminal charges is made by senior RUC officers on their assessment of the evidence which has been or may be obtained against the suspect. The decision whether or not to put the case forward for an interim custody order and eventual detention without trial, on the other hand, we believe, is one in which army intelligence officers play an important part in the sense that they are in a position to insist that a particular case be put before the Secretary of State recommending an interim custody order.

It is clear that the approach to suspects who are arrested and produced as a result of the army screening process is substantially different from that which is adopted in those cases in which the investigation of reported incidents or the arrest of suspects is wholly in the hands of the RUC. In these latter cases, we believe the "police prosecution" rather than the "military security" approach is followed, in that the whole process of questioning and investigation is directed towards the ultimate objective of proceedings in court rather than the possibility of detention without trial. The difference is, we believe, deeply rooted in the respective police and army attitudes to the control of terrorism and the training to which their officers are subjected. The army approach, we believe, lays most stress on the objective of putting IRA men, and to a lesser extent Protestant paramilitants, behind bars and is less concerned with the "technical" distinctions between conviction in court and detention without trial; the police approach, we believe, is centered on the traditional objective of proving a case against the suspect in a criminal court. This is not to say, of course, that a number of those arrested by the RUC are not "processed" in the joint army/RUC Special Branch interrogation centers and eventually held on interim custody orders with a view to detention, or that the traditional police approach is not affected by the present emergency conditions and procedures. But there remains, in our view, a substantial and important difference in the treatment of those suspects who are produced as a result of military and of police activity.

The difference in the army and police approaches to arrest and questioning is rendered even more significant by the fact that the army operates largely in Catholic and Republican areas, from which independent RUC activity is generally ruled out by local feelings, while the RUC operates with much greater freedom and efficacy in militant Protestant or mixed areas.

The practical results of this imbalance in army and police deployment are twofold. First, there is a difference in the nature of the security operation in the two communities. Catholic areas are subjected to what may be termed a communal screening process in which all young people are regarded as potential terrorists and treated accordingly, while in Protestant areas emphasis is placed on the investigation of specific incidents. Secondly, there is a resulting differential flow of suspects into the twin systems of court trial and administrative detention. This helps to explain the imbalance in the Republican and Loyalist population of the detention camps which has frequently been commented on. (In mid-1974 there were some five hundred Republican detainees compared with some fifty Loyalists, though the number of cases coming before the courts involving Loyalists and Republicans were roughly equal.) It should be emphasized that this differential treatment is not a result of deliberate discrimination or partiality on the part of either the army or the police, but stems from the different, perhaps in current conditions inevitably different, army and RUC deployment.

The broader effects on communal attitudes of this imbalance in the nature of the security operation in Catholic and Republican, and Protestant and Loyalist areas, respectively, is even more difficult to assess accurately and objectively. But there is no doubt, in our view, that it makes a substantial contribution to the continuing feeling in militant Republican areas that an element of unfair discrimination continues to exist in the treatment of IRA and Loyalist paramilitants. This feeling, we believe makes an important contribution to the efficacy of IRA propaganda and to the continuing pattern of recruitment to active terrorism on the Republican side which in its turn helps to promote reactive terrorism on the Loyalist side.

The conclusion which we would draw from this is a simple one, that the effect of the communal screening policy which the army has been permitted to pursue under the terms of the Emergency Provisions Act is counterproductive and should be replaced by a policy based on the investigation of individual incidents with a view to specific criminal proceedings. This, in our view, is what was in fact intended by the Diplock Committee. In simple terms, we believe that the "military security" approach should be superceded by the "police prosecution" approach.

Detention

The Diplock Committee justified the maintenance of a system of administrative detention of suspected terrorists primarily on the ground that the widespread intimidation of witnesses made it impossible to rely only on trials in ordinary criminal courts.

We are thus driven inescapably to the conclusion that until the current terrorism by extremist organizations of both factions in Northern Ireland can be eradicated, there will continue to be some dangerous terrorists against whom it will not be possible to obtain convictions by any form of criminal trial which we regard as appropriate to a court of law. . . . We are also driven inescapably to the conclusion that so long as these remain at liberty to operate in Northern Ireland it will not be possible to find witnesses prepared to testify against them in the criminal courts, except those serving in the army or the police, for whom effective protection can be provided. The dilemma is complete. The only hope of restoring the efficiency of criminal courts of law in Northern Ireland to deal with terrorist crimes is by using an extra-judicial process to deprive of their ability to operate in Northern Ireland, those terrorists whose activities result in the intimidation of witnesses [para. 27].

This conclusion, in the view of the Committee, would not be altered by the acceptance of the various recommendations which it made for alterations in existing rules of evidence and procedure to facilitate the conviction of guilty terrorists in the courts.

The essential difference between the internment of persons under the old Special Powers Act in Northern Ireland and the detention of terrorists under the Detention of Terrorists Order introduced in November 1972 is that, under the new procedure, the grounds for detention are more tightly drawn and the provisions for the quasi-judicial review of each case are formally independent of the executive. The final decision on continued detention under the old system lay with the Minister of Home Affairs at Stormont, while under the new system it rests with the commissioners appointed under the Emergency Provisions Act.

Interim Custody Orders

An interim custody order is normally made against a suspected terrorist after his arrest and detention for the seventy-two-hour period permitted by Section 12 of the Emergency Provisions Act. The formal grounds on which such an order may be made by the ministers of the Northern Ireland Office are that the person is "suspected of having been concerned in the commission or attempted commission of any act of terrorism or in the direction, organization or training of persons for the purpose of terrorism." Soon after the introduction of the new procedure in November 1972, the Secretary of State, we have reason to believe, issued guidelines to the security forces setting out the way in which he would interpret this power so that only those cases which met his requirements would be submitted for his consideration. The substance of these guidelines, we believe, is that a number of separate traces must be produced against the suspect indicating his involvement in terrorist activities. Some sources have reported that at least six such traces must be produced. A trace for this purpose may range from some kind of direct evidence that the suspect has been involved in a specific terrorist act, as for instance an alleged identification which the witness is not willing to confirm in court, to circumstantial evidence, as for instance the presence of the suspect in the vicinity of the incident, to the most tenuous indication of involvement, as for instance association with other "known" terrorists. Most frequently the principal traces will be the statement of an informer, perhaps supplemented by one or two other circumstantial and indirect traces to make up the required number. It should be stressed that there is no statutory basis for this system of counting traces.

A further significant aspect of the interim custody order procedure, as we understand it, is that no action on the part of the police is necessary either in recommending or commenting on the case made out to the Secretary of State. This means in practice that the army intelligence officers in Northern Ireland have an entirely independent channel of communication to the Secretary of State, which may be used to ensure the continued detention of any person against whom they can produce the necessary list of traces. There have been reports that on occasions there has been disagreement between the army and the RUC on whether a particular suspect should in fact be recommended for an interim custody order. Whether this is true or not, however, it is clear that the existence of this separate channel is an important part of the whole "military security" approach to terrorism in which much less attention is directed than in the "police prosecution" approach to the proof of specific criminal acts.

A final important aspect of the interim custody order procedure, as it is operated in practice, is the fact that in most cases the suspect is held for a good deal longer than the twenty-eight days specified in the Detention of Terrorists Order. To legalize the extension of custody beyond that period, it is necessary for a senior police officer to make a formal reference of the case for determination by a commissioner, but there is no reason to believe that this is regarded as more than a formality. Many suspects are held on interim custody orders for periods of five or six months or longer pending the hearing of their cases. The practical effect of the existing system is thus to give the security forces, and in particular the army, the power to arrest and imprison a suspect for around six months without any independent judicial consideration of the case. In view of the large proportion of cases in which the commissioners reject the case made out by the security forces and order the release of the suspect, as will be seen, this is, in our view, a matter of grave concern. It is also, we believe, an important part of the "military security" approach to terrorism in which putting suspected terrorists behind bars is an end in itself.

It is difficult to give a clear statistical base to the picture of the interim custody order procedure which has just been outlined, since the security forces were unwilling (until recently) to issue regular statistics on the use which they have made of their powers in this respect. There is no information, for instance, on how many cases referred to the Northern Ireland Office for consideration are accepted and how many are rejected. But we have been able to construct a table of the number of interim custody orders actually made, the various forms of release and the net total of persons detained at any given date.

The most significant feature of this analysis, as shown in Table 14-1, is the level of military activity in terms of the number of new interim custody orders made in each period. The figures show clearly that the rate of new orders declined from a maximum of just over fifty per month in the first half of 1973 to thirty-six per month in the second half of 1973 and a mere eighteen per month in the first two months of 1974; when the new Labour administration took over, the rate increased again to thirty-four per month. Despite these variations, however, the terminal figures of the total numbers of persons held in custody remained remarkably constant from the early part of 1973 to the present. Given the commitment of various secretaries of state to reducing the numbers detained, it is scarcely surprising that the public has become somewhat skeptical about such undertakings. There is at least some ground for suggesting on these figures that the system of detention without trial has a momentum of its own, in the sense that the flow of releases tends to be fully offset by the number of new interim custody orders.

Commissioners' Hearings

The figures for the results of initial commissioners' hearings, as set out in Table 14-1, show clearly that the commissioners are very far from being mere rubber stamps for executive decisions. After the initial period between January and June 1973, when many of the cases heard concerned those who had been arrested and detained under the old Special Powers Act procedure, the proportion of releases ordered by the commissioners has remained roughly constant at one third. Various interpretations may be put on this fact. An acquittal rate of one in three of all cases in ordinary criminal court proceedings would certainly be regarded as highly abnormal and as a ground for considering

Table 14-1
Hearings Figures for the Operation of the Northern Ireland System of Detection of Terrorists under the Detection of Terrorists Order, 1972, and the Emergency Provisions Act, 1973, for Selected Periods

Period	No of New ICOs Made (est.)	Commissioners' Hearings						Released by Sec. of State	Died & Escaped	Total in custody at start and at end period	
		Initial Hearings		Appeal Hearings		Review Hearings					
		Total	Released	Total	Released	Total	Released			Start	End
Jan-June 1973	309	371	55 15%	27	7 26%	—	—	8	3	292	528
July-Dec 1973	208	117	41 35%	31	5 16%	73	26 36%	66	4	528	595
Jan-Feb 1974	36	50	15 30%	9	1 11%	45	23 51%	3	1	593	586
Mar-July 1974	170	134	48 35%	61	5 8%	184	81 44%	32	2	586	589
Aug-Oct 1974	53	94	34 36%	19	5 26%	75	28 37%	41	(2)	589	535

whether the prosecuting authorities were properly performing their duties. The high discharge rate in the commissioners' hearings, in our view, should be regarded in the same light, as an indication of the weakness of the case produced against many of the persons against whom an interim custody order is made, rather than as an indication of what a good safeguard the system of hearings represents. The fact that the security authorities have continued to present cases for the commissioners' determination with such a high failure rate is an indication, in our view, of the extent to which traditional legal values have been eroded by the pursuit of what we have termed the "military security" approach. The additional fact that the representatives of many of those against whom detention orders are made remain unconvinced, on the evidence which has been revealed to them, that a case has been satisfactorily established against their client in accordance with the terms of the Detention of Terrorists Order is a further cause for concern.

We have not been able to establish any precise relationship between the system of review hearings and the exercise of the ministerial power of intervention. But there is some reason to believe, on the evidence of the figures in Table 14-1, that a high level of ministerial releases does result in a lower proportion of releases in review hearings. There is nothing surprising or improper about this. Since likely candidates for release are selected primarily by the security authorities, it is to be expected that, in a period when they are required to produce a list of names for release by ministerial direction, the proportion of cases dealt with by way of regular review hearings in which the security authorities make no objection to release will decline. But the overlap in jurisdiction in this respect, in conjunction with the abandonment of the notion that the length of detention should be related to the seriousness of the suspect's alleged involvement, further reduces the likelihood of general public understanding or acceptance of the system of commissioners' hearings as a whole.

Conclusions

Our conclusion from this review of the operation of the Detention of Terrorists Order is that the system has been systematically abused in pursuit of what we have called the "military security" approach to terrorism. By this we mean that large numbers of those channelled through the system have been relatively unimportant members or adherents of terrorist organizations. The primary evidence for this is the very high rate of releases ordered by the commissioners. We are also concerned about the fact that many of those whose release is ordered have already spent some six months or so in detention. The security authorities appear to have adopted the view that there is more to be gained from putting large numbers of suspected terrorists behind bars than is lost by the risk of unjustified detention in a number of cases.

The ill effects of this policy, in our view, are substantially increased by the differential application of the military security and police prosecution approaches in Catholic and Protestant areas respectively. The reality of this difference is borne out by the figures released by the security authorities. In May 1974 it was reported that, of some 1,500 terrorists in custody, both convicted and detained, 290 were convicted Loyalists. At the same time, the figure for Loyalists under detention was approximately 60, out of a total number detained of some 600. This means that while the Loyalists constituted almost one-fifth of those held under court sentences, they constituted only one-tenth of the number detained. This variation, in our view, is not the result of differences in the extent of intimidation in Protestant and Catholic areas, but of the different methods which are employed by the police and army in the pursuit of terrorists.

There is no reason to believe that there are now any persons held in detention who have not been in some way involved or associated with terrorism. But many of those held are, in our view, "small fish" who have been dragged into the net as the result of the military security approach. In this sense, the system has been operated in an entirely different way from that which we believe was intended by the Diplock Committee, which emphasized that only those against whom there was material which would carry complete conviction as to guilt to any impartial observer should be dealt with in the extra-judicial system (para. 28).

We have considered whether any further safeguards might be introduced to enable a better discrimination to be made between those whose detention might be justifiable and those whose detention is, in our view, not justifiable, as for instance by setting a numerical limit on the number of persons who may be lawfully held without trial. But we have finally been forced back to the conclusion that no system which does not preserve the majority of the procedural and evidential safeguards of the common-law can effectively protect the individual from injustice or guarantee that the emergency detention procedure as a whole will not be abused.

Summary of Findings

The main findings of this survey of the operation of the Northern Ireland (Emergency Provisions) Act 1973 may be summarized as follows.

First, there is evidence that the procedure for arrest and questioning and for extra-judicial detention has been abused. The security authorities have in some areas mounted a "dredging" operation based on widespread screening. This has resulted, in our view, in large numbers of wholly innocent persons being arrested and large numbers whose involvement in terrorist activities is relatively unimportant being detained. We are concerned about the way in which the army has made use of the powers provided in Sections 12 and 16 of the Act, which in our view does not correspond with the intentions of the Diplock Committee. We are also concerned about the continuing high level of releases ordered in commissioners' hearings, which in our view is an indication of the weakness of the grounds on which many suspects are being held, often for periods of up to six months. The fact that a "military security" approach to terrorism, in which the main emphasis is on putting suspected terrorists behind bars, has been operated principally in Catholic and Republican areas, while a "police prosecution" approach, in which the main emphasis is on the proof of specific criminal charges against suspects, is generally applied in Protestant and Loyalist areas is a further cause for concern. This difference in approach, in our view, has resulted in the relative imbalance in the number of Republican and Loyalist suspects dealt with in the courts and by extra-judicial detention.

Secondly, there is evidence that the system of Diplock trials has worked well. The suspension of jury trials appears to have removed a major source of differentiation between Protestant and Catholic defendants, though there is some danger on the evidence of our survey of an increasing readiness on the part of judges to accept prosecution evidence. The provisions on the shifting of the burden of proof in possession of firearms cases have worked well in the sense that the judges have been free to decide on the evidence as to the guilt or innocence of the accused, untrammelled by legal technicalities. We are less happy about the operation of the provisions permitting the admission in evidence of certain confessions that have not been voluntarily given in accordance with ordinary common-law rules. In respect of the selection of charges, we are satisfied that the prosecuting authorities have acted fairly in relation to both Protestant and Catholic defendants. In respect of sentencing, while there has been widespread variation, this has in our view been due to the different circumstances of particular cases rather than to any form of sectarian bias. The only cause for concern in this respect, in our view, is the apparent difference in judicial perception of the IRA and of Protestant paramilitary associations and the related difference in approach to their habitual weapons, rifles, and handguns, respectively.

Thirdly, there is evidence from our small survey of public attitudes that the assumptions on which the Diplock Committee based its recommendations of a two-pronged system of criminal trials and extra-judicial detention are incorrect. In the first place there was widespread dissatisfaction, expressed by half the Protestant and almost all the Catholic respondents, with the system of extra-judicial detention as such. There was also evidence of more general lack of confidence in the judicial system as a whole stemming from this dissatisfaction, and of a commitment among members of both majority and minority communities to the values embodied in the common-law conception of trial by due process of law.

The Alternative to Detention

The conclusion which we draw from these findings is that the maintenance of a system of extra-judicial detention is unacceptable, in terms both of the risk of abuse and of the serious effect on public confidence in the judicial system and in the maintenance of law and order in general. The only way of avoiding both individual injustice and the use of the system of emergency powers as a whole, in our view, is to rely on the safeguards which have been developed in the common-law tradition for precisely that purpose.

Accordingly, we recommend the extended use of the system of Diplock trials in combination with what we have called the "police prosecution" approach under which suspects are arrested and questioned and eventually charged and tried only in respect of specific offenses. To make this alternative fully effective in the present emergency conditions, however, we recommend a number of further changes in that part of the Emergency Provisions Act which deals with the trial of scheduled offenses.

In the first place, we consider that Section 5 of the Act should be amended to permit the admission in evidence of signed statements made to a senior police officer where by reason of fear or intimidation the person making the statement is unwilling to appear in court. Such a limitation on the right of cross-examination, which the Diplock Committee held to be an essential element in a criminal trial, is in our view an acceptable price to pay for giving added efficacy to the courts in conditions of fear and intimidation. The requirement that the statement be taken before a senior police officer should prove sufficient protection against the poor quality and reliability of many informer's statements currently being admitted at commissioners' hearings. A derogation from Article 6 of the European Convention on Human Rights and Fundamental Freedoms in this respect is, in our view, infinitely preferable to the maintenance of a "purer" form of criminal trial in conjunction with a system of extra-judicial detention.

Secondly, we recommend that it should be made a criminal offense to "be concerned in the commission or attempted commission of any act of terrorism, or in the direction, organization or training of others for that purpose." This formulation has been taken directly from the Diplock Committee and the Emergency Provisions Act. We have considered whether the more widespread use of charges of membership in an illegal organization, which our survey showed to have been used as independent grounds for criminal prosecution in only a handful of cases, would fulfill the same purpose, but are satisfied that the difficulty of satisfactorily proving membership and of ensuring that the correct organizations are rendered illegal, particularly on the Loyalist side, makes the Diplock formulation preferable. It is also preferable, in our view, to an attempt to make use of more general conspiracy charges. We have no doubt that there would be general agreement that the kind of conduct covered by the formulation we have suggested is worthy of criminal prohibition, and are satisfied that the criminal courts can deal adequately with charges of such an offense in the light of the evidence put before them.

Thirdly, with a view to increasing and maintaining public confidence in the decisions of Diplock courts, we recommend that a panel of lay assessors be appointed to sit with the judges dealing with scheduled offenses. In view of the pressure on the judiciary as a whole and the desirability of maintaining some measure of public involvement in the working of the courts, we would prefer a system of trial by a single judge and assessors to the alternative of trial by a bench of judges. The jurisdiction of assessors should not extend to sentencing.

Our remaining recommendations follow directly from the view that the "police prosecution" approach to terrorist offenses should be adopted, and that the ordinary procedural safeguards of the common law are the only effective protection against the risk of injustice or abuse.

Fourthly, we recommend that suspected terrorists should be arrestable only on reasonable suspicion of having been involved in specific terrorist incidents.

Fifthly, we recommend that while the interrogation of those reasonably suspected of terrorist offenses should be permitted, formal administrative rules should be published stating the conditions under which such interrogation is permitted, and that a panel of lay visitors should have access at all times to interrogation centers.

Sixthly, we recommend the regular publication of figures on the operation of all aspects of the Emergency Provisions Act, in particular those concerning the arrest and questioning of suspects.

Notes

Notes

Chapter 1
Definitions and Dimensions of Terrorism

1. M. Cherif Bassiouni, ed., *International Terrorism and Political Crimes* (Springfield, Ill.: Charles C. Thomas, 1975), 594 pp.

2. Ibid., Appendix R or S, pp. 557-63 and 573-79, respectively.

3. Algeria, Congo, Democratic Yemen, Guinea, India, Mauritania, Nigeria, Syrian Arab Republic, Tunisia, United Republic of Tanzania, Yemen, Yugoslavia, Zaire, and Zambia.

4. See Bassiouni, *International Terrorism*, Appendix S, pp. 564-65 and 569-71.

5. For more on this point, see Brian M. Jenkins, "International Terrorism: A New Mode of Conflict," Paper presented at the fifth course of the International School on Disarmament and Research on Conflicts, held at the Collegio Universitario in Urbino, Italy, August 12-14, 1974, 48 pp.

6. Some countries, e.g., France and the United States, have undergone revolution, but have since become established to the point where they belong to the former group. Other countries, e.g., the USSR, also founded on the basis of revolution and also established to the point of being concerned by disruptive activities of internal "dissidents," clearly do not fit neatly into this scheme.

7. See W.W. Minor, "Skyjacking Crime Control Models," *Journal of Criminal Law and Criminology* 66 (1975):94-105.

8. Brian M. Jenkins, "High Technology Terrorism and Surrogate War: The Impact of New Technology on Low-level Violence" (Santa Monica, Calif.: The Rand Paper Series, 1975), 26 pp.

9. L.C. Green, "The Nature and Control of International Terrorism," Occasional Paper 1, Department of Political Science, University of Alberta, Edmonton, 1974, p. 10.

10. Jenkins, "International Terrorism," discusses this point further.

11. See "Final Document: Conclusions and Recommendations," in Bassiouni, *International Terrorism,* Part II, Section 6, pp. xviii-xix.

Chapter 2
The Issue of Prevention

1. L.C. Green, "The Nature and Control of International Terrorism," Occasional Paper 1, Department of Political Science, University of Alberta, Edmonton, 1974.

2. See W.W. Minor, "Skyjacking Crime Control Models," *Journal of Criminal Law and Criminology* 66 (1975):94-105.

3. Robert L. Hamblin and Jerry L.L. Miller, "Mathematical Analyses and Theory of Air-hijacking Epidemics: A Preliminary Report," mimeographed, University of Arizona, Tuscon (undated), 34 pp.

4. Ibid., p. 3.

5. Minor, "Skyjacking Crime Control Models," provides an excellent analysis of the history of skyjacking control in the United States.

6. Oscar Newman, *Defensible Space: Crime Prevention through Urban Design* (New York: Collier Books, 1973), 264 pp.

7. The role of environmental design in crime prevention has attracted considerable attention in recent years. A crime prevention workshop, held in Toronto, devoted one out of five discussion groups to the question of environmental design and modification. The other four topics were medical intervention, community involvement, police involvement, and law reform. See Diane MacFarlane, ed., *A Crime Prevention Workshop: Report of the Proceedings* (Toronto: Centre of Criminology, University of Toronto, 1975), 144 pp.

8. Ibid., p. 139.

9. Ibid.

10. Richard Clutterbuck, *Living with Terrorism* (London: Faber and Faber, 1975), 160 pp.

11. Green, "The Nature and Control of International Terrorism."

12. Ibid., p. 49.

13. Brian M. Jenkins, "International Terrorism: A New Mode of Conflict," Paper presented at the fifth course of the International School on Disarmament and Research on Conflicts, held at the Collegio Universitario in Urbino, Italy, August 12-14, 1974, p. 20.

14. Minor, "Skyjacking Crime Control Models."

Chapter 3
The Impact of the Response to Terrorism

1. W.W. Minor, "Skyjacking Crime Control Models," *Journal of Criminal Law and Criminology* 66 (1975).

2. Louk H.C. Hulsman, "The Penal System as a Social Problem," Text of address given at Wingspread Conference, "Rural Criminal Justice: Issues and Answers," Collegeville, Minnesota, May 3, 1974, p. 1.

3. Austin MacCormick, quoted in Massachusetts Correctional Association, *Correctional Reform: Illusion and Reality,* Correctional Research Bulletin No. 22 (Boston, 1972), p. 26.

4. Richard Clutterbuck, *Living with Terrorism* (London: Faber and Faber, 1975), 160 pp.

5. Robert L. Hamblin and Jerry L.L. Miller, "Mathematical Analyses and Theory of Air-hijacking Epidemics: A Preliminary Report," mimeographed, University of Arizona, Tuscon (undated), 34 pp.

6. See Minor, "Skyjacking Crime Control Models."

7. See Clutterbuck, *Living with Terrorism,* p. 22, re Marighela.

8. Yehezkel Dror, "T.F.B. (Terror, Fanaticism, Blackmail) as a Strategic Problem," Discussion paper prepared for Symposium on Terrorism, Pre-emption and Surprise, sponsored by the Leonard Davis Institute of International Relations at the Hebrew University, Jerusalem, June 1975, 9 pp.

9. Gregory Bateson, personal communication to R.D. Crelinsten.

Chapter 8
Prevention, Legislation, and Research Pertaining to Terrorism in Belgium

1. *Moniteur Belge,* August 15, 1973, p. 9309.

2. *Moniteur Belge,* July 24, 1975.

3. The European Commission on Human Rights is a possible model that could be used for such a purpose.

4. See also the E.E.C. Court in Luxembourg and the prejudicial question.

Chapter 11
The Antiterrorist Legislation in Sweden

1. See further Jacob Sundberg, "Recent Changes in Swedish Family Law," *American Journal of Comparative Law* 23 (1975):42 and note 28.

2. See further Jacob Sundberg, "Piracy: Air and Sea," Chapter IX, Section 1 in *A Treatise on International Criminal Law,* vol. 1, *Crimes and Punishment,* ed. by M. Cherif Bassiouni and Ved P. Nanda (Springfield, Ill.: Charles C. Thomas, 1973), p. 478 f.

3. Göran Melander, "Flyktingar och asyl," (Stockholm: Norstedts, 1972), p. 49; cf. 47 f.

4. *Statens Offentliga Utredningar* 85 (1972):19 f.; Melander, "Flyktingar och asyl," p. 43.

5. Melander, "Flyktingar och asyl," p. 70.

6. *Kungl. Proposition*, 109 (1971):4.

7. *Statens Offentliga Utredningar* 84 (1972):141.

8. *Annual of Power and Conflict* (London: Institute for the Study of Conflict, 1973-74), p. 8.

9. This governmental agency went to the extent of printing anticoup posters for local distribution in Sweden.

10. See Terri Shaw, *International Herald Tribune,* January 8, 1974, p. 3.

11. For years, some 2,000 Cubans have reportedly been working on aid primarily in African countries but also in Southern Yemen and Vietnam. See *International Herald Tribune,* January 24-25, 1976, p. 2; cf. issue 2, January

1976, p. 1. The size of the Cuban military expeditionary force to Angola had risen to some 7,500 men by the end of 1975; official confirmation of the intervention was given by Premier Fidel Castro, December 18, 1975. See *International Herald Tribune,* December 20-21, 1975, p. 1.

12. "Handläggningen av säkerhetsfragor," in *Statens Offentliga Utredningar* 4 (1968).

13. For a scholarly report on the matter, see Moshe Ma'oz, "Soviet and Chinese Relations with the Palestinian Guerilla Organizations," *Jerusalem Papers on Peace Problems* 4 (March 1974).

14. Quote as per the official ombudsman report [hereinafter cited as JO only] (1973), p. 52 f. Translation mine.

15. JO (1973), p. 87.

16. JO (1973), p. 72; JO (1975-76), p. 160 f.

17. JO (1973), p. 90.

18. JO (1975-76), p. 167.

19. In connection with the removal of the Yugoslav minister of the interior, Radovan Stijacic, his resort to provocative tactics came to light. The Belgrade periodical *Nin,* attempting muckraking, in 1973 reportedly disclosed materials suggesting that Hrkac had had status of *agent provocateur;* see report in the Stockholm daily *Expressen,* October 14, 1973, p. 13.

20. JO (1973), p. 48.

21. As per report by Sune Olsson in *Svenska Dagbladet,* September 23, 1972.

22. The last independent daily, *Göteborgs Handels och Sjöfartstidning,* closed on September 8, 1973. Its editor-in-chief, Björn Ahlander, attracted general attention by an unsuccessful attempt to control his leftist "cultural" editor who expanded into general politics. Ahlander's demise was speeded up by the attacks against him that were administered by the future, supposedly "conservative," editor-in-chief of *Svenska Dagbladet.*

23. See article by Sune Olsson in *Svenska Dagbladet,* September 23, 1972. The leftist infiltration of the paper, crowned by a poster set up on the door to the foreign editor's office reading "USA Out of Vietnam," took place between 1968 and 1972. It was made possible principally by means of a new administrative director's edging out the old guard and recruiting young leftists from the journalist school (*Journalisthögskolan*) that had been taken over by the leftists right after its creation and converted into a school of socialist indoctrination. The reorientation first showed in headlines and picture texts and later crept into the very texts of articles and notes. The editor's page was the last to go.

24. *Ds Ju* 35 (1972), reprinted in *Kungl. Proposition* 37 (1973):20-116.

25. ICAO Document 8966. It did not enter into force until January 26, 1973; the Swedish instruments of ratification were deposited on July 10, 1973. See *Sveriges Överenskommelser med främmande makter,* no. 48 (1973).

26. *Sveriges Överenskommelser med främmende makter* [hereinafter SO], no. 26 (1952).

27. JO (1975-76), p. 168.

28. *Expressen,* February 13, 1973.

29. The "double-think" of Elwin is, of course, not accidental. In allegiance to the Marxist faith in predetermined progression, he sees everything "rightist" as "criminal" and everything "leftist" as legitimate.

30. *Dagens Nyheter,* February 3, 1973.

31. *Expressen,* February 19, 1973.

32. *Expressen,* February 24, 1973.

33. *Expressen,* February 19, 1973.

34. *Expressen* February 24, 1973.

35. Cf. Nils Beckman, *Scandinavian Studies in Law* (1963):16 f.

36. *Expressen,* February 19, 1973.

37. *Dagens Nyheter,* February 3, 1973.

38. See further, Jacob Sundberg, "Thinking the Unthinkable or the Case of Dr. Tsironis," Chapter V, section 4 in *International Terrorism and Political Crimes,* ed. by M. Cherif Bassiouni (Springfield, Ill.: Charles C. Thomas, 1975), p. 458.

39. Ibid., p. 451 and note 11.

40. *The Daily Star* (Beirut), September 23, 1974.

41. "Japanese Terrorist Group Moves Around," *International Herald Tribune,* September 16, 1974.

42. Göran Melander, *Terroristlagen: ett onödigt ont* (Stockholm: Bokförlaget Pan/Norstedts, 1975), p. 34.

43. *Arrêts du Tribunal Fédéral Suisse* 87-I-134.

44. *Proposition* 18 (1975-76):151.

45. Ibid., p. 207.

46. *Proposition* 18 (1975-76):151; *Proposition* 72 (1975):11.

47. *Proposition* 18 (1975-76):151.

48. The newspaper story was more dramatic. It claimed that in December 1974 the Japanese government asked the Swedish security police to find and arrest Kyoichi Shimada, believed to be the mastermind behind the Lydda massacre, who had taken refuge in Sweden after the wrecking of a plan to seize the Japanese Embassy in Oslo, Norway. When the Swedish service failed to find Shimada, the Japanese government secured Swedish permission to send three Japanese security agents to Sweden for the search. Then Mabuchi sent his circular letter.

49. See *International Herald Tribune,* September 8, 1975, pp. 1, 5.

50. *Time Magazine,* August 18, 1975, p. 18.

51. Melander, *Terroristlagen: ett onödigt ont,* p. 102 f.; cf. 45.

52. For a full discussion, see ibid., p. 103. Cf. Frede Castberg, *The European Convention on Human Rights* (Leiden: Sijthoff/Oceana, 1974), p. 177.

53. Överaklågaren i Stockholm dnr OÅ Ad I 493-72, comments of January 9, 1973, signed L. Hiort.

54. Right after the attack on the embassy, *Dagens Nyheter* published a major attack on the Federal Republic in three consecutive articles written by Dr. Frank Hirschfeldt, which subsequently were made the basis of much anti-German comment in other leftist mass media. See *Dagens Nyheter,* April 22, 23, and 27, 1975.

55. Melander, "Flyktingar och asyl," p. 65.

Chapter 12
Political Prisoners and Terrorists in American
Correctional Institutions

1. American extradition law prohibits the extradition of persons charged with political offenses; the term *political offense* generally means a crime against a government.

2. See James W.L. Park, "The Organization of Prison Violence," paper presented at the Conference on Prison Violence, University of New Hampshire, Durham, Summer 1975.

3. See Lawrence A. Bennett, "The Study of Violence in California Prisons," paper presented at the Conference on Prison Violence, University of New Hampshire, Durham, Summer 1975.

4. See John P. Conrad, "The Beast Behind the Wall," paper presented at the Conference on Prison Violence, University of New Hampshire, Durham, Summer 1975.

5. See Park, "The Organization of Prison Violence."

6. National Advisory Commission on Criminal Justice Standard and Goals, *Corrections* (Washington, D.C.: U.S. Government Printing Office, 1973).

Chapter 13
Terrorism and Criminal Justice Operations in the
Federal Republic of Germany

1. Wolfgang D. Salewski, *"Luftpiraterie: Verlauf, Verhalten, Hintergründe,"* mimeographed, PPM Salewski, Munich (undated), 70 pp.

Index

Index

About the Contributors

Inkeri Anttila is director of the Research Institute of Legal Policy, attached to the Ministry of Justice, Helsinki, Finland.

Kevin Boyle is a barrister and also lecturer in law at Queen's University in Belfast, Northern Ireland.

Erich Corves is assistant deputy minister of justice in the Federal Republic of Germany.

Bart de Schutter is director of the International Criminal Law Centre, University of Brussels, Brussels, Belgium.

Edith Flynn is professor at the School of Criminal Justice, Northeastern University, Boston, U.S.A.

Tom Hadden is a barrister and also lecturer in law at Queen's University in Belfast, Northern Ireland.

Paddy Hillyard is lecturer in social administration at the New University of Ulster, Coleraine, Northern Ireland.

Jacques Léauté is director of the Institute of Criminology, Université de Paris, Paris, France.

Jacob Sundberg is professor at the Law School, University of Stockholm, Stockholm, Sweden.

About the Authors

Ronald D. Crelinsten is a research associate with the International Centre for Comparative Criminology of the Université de Montréal, where he has organized a series of international seminars devoted to the subject of terrorism and hostage taking. He is also professor of Humanities at Vanier College in Montréal, where he teaches courses on the social impact of dichotomous thinking and the role of perception and beliefs in everyday conceptions of reality. He received the B.Sc. in genetics from McGill University and the M.Sc. in biopsychology from the University of Chicago and has received fellowships from the Quebec Ministry of Education and the University of Chicago. He has coauthored, with Professor Szabo, a book on hostage taking that is forthcoming.

Danielle Laberge-Altmejd is a doctoral candidate in the School of Criminology at the Université de Montréal, where she also received the B.Sc. and M.Sc. She has done research, organized seminars, and published articles mainly in the fields of juvenile delinquency and social reaction to deviance. She has also served as research consultant for the Quebec Ministry of Social Affairs, and has received fellowships from the Quebec Ministry of Education and the Canada Council.

Denis Szabo is a Fellow of the Royal Society of Canada, professor at the Université de Montréal and Director of the International Centre for Comparative Criminology. He attended the Universities of Budapest, Louvain, and Paris. He obtained his doctorate in social and political science at the University of Louvain and his diploma in criminology at the Sorbonne. He taught at the Universities of Louvain, Lyon, and Paris and, since 1958, has been teaching at the Université de Montréal. The author of many works and scientific articles, he has also been a visiting professor and lecturer in numerous universities in America, Europe, Africa, and Asia. He is an Officer of the National Order of the Ivory Coast and recipient of scientific distinctions from several learned societies, as well as a member of a number of American and European scientific societies. He is vice president of the International Society of Criminology.

Mohsen Alhaj

Steff Harper.